A Better Version of You

A Life-Changing Guide to Personal and
Professional Fulfillment

Victoria,
I'm so excited to see
you grow & stregthen
this year!
Martha

Martha Karelius

ISBN: 151412209X
ISBN 13: 9781514122099
Library of Congress Control Number: 2015908739
CreateSpace Independent Publishing Platform
North Charleston, South Carolina

*To my husband, John, who lives and
breathes self-organization,
and who, by doing so, enjoys a rewarding,
self-actualized life.*

Contents

Introduction

> "Go confidently in the direction of your
> dreams. Live the life you've imagined.
> As you simplify your life, the laws of the
> universe will be simpler."

> — Henry David Thoreau (1854)

Time management is as elusive to modern man as that pot of gold at the end of the rainbow. I believe that the concept of managing or controlling time is a fallacy. We can only manage or control what we do with that time. My focus is to do the little things every day that move me closer to my goals. This might be spending time with family and friends, building my career, learning something new, or pursuing fun adventures and personal hobbies. As an example, at the height of my career I was the number-two agent in the United States for CENTURY 21. That same year I managed the number-seven office in the CENTURY 21 system, 120 agents strong. I was a member of two book clubs and a quilting club. I visited my son in Germany when he completed his tour in Iraq, spent a week at a cooking school in Italy, and celebrated New Year's in Japan with my daughter. And so it can be said, and in fact it has been said, that I am very good at time management. I appreciate that, but I think it takes more than managing time. I feel my success lies in excellent self-organization.

Not that long ago news traveled only as fast as it could be physically shared. Neighbors chatted over back fences and employees exchanged juicy tidbits at the water cooler. Today we can transmit verbal information and data to the far corners of the earth at the speed of light. Consider the way our daily lives have changed in recent years with regard to mail. For the longest time it was delivered to our homes once a day, every day except Sunday. If we worked in an office, it was delivered once a day, weekdays, as well. The entire process required a mere few minutes and had a start and a finish. Circulars and ads went directly into the trash. The bills went into one stack and personal cards or letters were read and cherished. Done.

Today mail pops into our inbox relentlessly, 24/7. It has become such a distraction that it is possible to lose an entire day checking and responding to e-mail. We get involved in e-mail conversations that volley back and forth ending with a series of parting words, including a few "have a nice days." It's as if no one wants to be the first to hang up. Eventually someone sends a happy face emoticon and the e-mail thread finally ends.

While you're checking (and rechecking) your e-mail, you receive a message to alert you that someone has commented on a photo you are tagged in on Facebook. Curious about that photo, you follow the link to the post only to find that you aren't actually in the photo—just tagged. But while you're there…

And so it goes.

The distractions are relentless. How will we ever have time to follow our hopes and dreams or do the things that make our hearts sing if we can't even keep up with our mail? We will do it through self-organization. This starts with excellent personal goals and thoughtful daily plans. We will learn to prioritize and hold ourselves accountable. In other words, we will run our lives instead of chasing our tails, and by doing so, live the self-actualized life we have imagined.

In this book I will share a number of ideas that work for me. My hope is that some of these concepts resonate with you. Try them out, adjust as necessary, and implement the systems that you feel will make you a better version of the person you were yesterday. There is no one right way to live life. By forming good habits and living in a purposeful way, we can enjoy a richer, more fulfilling existence. And that is our pot of gold at the end of the rainbow.

One

Be the Real Deal

"Always be a first-rate version of yourself and
not a second-rate version of someone else."

— Judy Garland (1988)

Feel free to be your authentic self. We acknowledge that nobody's perfect, so let's agree to lower the bar on perfectionism. Not every day is the best day ever. You don't have to be perfect to be positive, forward thinking, and human. It's OK to admit that you can't be everything everyone needs you to be, and do everything that needs to be done, all the time. We try not to make mistakes, but we do. If we are genuine, transparent, and human, we can't go too far wrong.

When I was growing up, children were expected to be "seen and not heard." We were told that boys did not cry, and even on bad days, my mother was expected to put on a happy face for my father when he came home from work. After all, he held down a real job. No wonder we struggle with authenticity. From our very early years, we are trained to rein in our emotions and adopt a slightly altered version of our true selves.

Many people are afraid to let their guard down because they don't want to appear vulnerable. Being vulnerable somehow implies that we are weak. We are most comfortable demonstrating that we are capable and confident even in situations where we are in totally over our heads. For example, when shopping I'm usually on a mission to find something specific or something for an "occasion." My default answer when a salesperson offers assistance is, "No, thank you. Just looking." Because I do need help, regret sets in as soon as the words come out. It's as if accepting help from someone who specializes in customer service is a disgrace. We aren't required to have all the answers, and allowing an expert to guide us is not only smart, but much more efficient than wasting time trying to figure things out for ourselves. There is nothing wrong with being authentic and admitting that we could use a little help. Knowing where to go to get the answers is the next best thing to having them.

I have a tendency to buy the same clothes year in and year out. It's a running joke shared with my daughter. If we are shopping together, or I text a photo of something that catches my eye, her response is usually, "Don't you already own that?" I usually do. Perhaps not literally, but I am admittedly stuck in a clothing rut. There's a reason for that. It's just me.

I was invited to a retreat in Lake Arrowhead with about fifteen very powerful, confident women. It was intimidating and inspiring at the same time. A few of the ladies hit the boutiques for a little shopping fun and discovered a silk jacket made of very bold, bright-red/orange prints. It was quite a work of art. They agreed that the jacket should represent the new, vibrant me and they persuaded me to buy it. The minute the purchase was complete, buyer's remorse set in. The jacket was definitely not me and it never left the hanger. Frankly, whenever I put it on, it felt like it was "wearing" me. I'm simply not the bright, bold person they wanted me to be. I prefer tailored, unpretentious clothes and accept the fact that trendy, fun, exotic, or otherwise interesting clothing doesn't work for me. I'm fine with that and agree with Ralph Waldo Emerson that "to be yourself in a world that is constantly trying to make you something else is the greatest accomplishment."

Brene Brown wrote a best-selling book about being vulnerable, called Daring Greatly. In it, she talks about life events that make people feel vulnerable. Getting a promotion and not being sure you are capable of the job, getting fired, falling in love, waiting for results from medical tests, asking for forgiveness, or reaching out to someone who has suffered a loss are just a few of the scenarios we dread. She makes an excellent point when she says that when we are going through something uncomfortable, like one of the situations above, we feel weak and vulnerable. When we see others in the same circumstances, we think of them as strong and courageous. We need to give ourselves a break.

Toward the end of my real estate career, I had several friends who were retired and encouraged me to do the same. They tried to sell me on the idea by telling me that they wake up every morning with "no agenda." Additionally, according to them, being retired keeps you extremely busy. I am very happy for them that they are at peace and enjoying their lives. The difference between us is that I prefer to wake up with a purpose and don't want to be "busy." I want to be valuable, to make a difference, and to give back.

With that in mind, I decided to start my own business by drawing on my depth of knowledge amassed over many years in real estate. I named the business A Better Version of You. Sound familiar? Not knowing exactly what my focus would be, my options were kept open by selecting a name that would cover a number of topics. I was considering mentoring real estate agents, but decided that there are a number of excellent choices readily available. I also considered creating seminars and workshops for women to help them cope with the challenge of balancing family and career. The options were narrowing, but had not yet crystallized.

A Better Version of You made me a better version of me--real, down to earth, and relatable. It was gratifying to see the business unfold the way I had imagined. Everyone was receptive and offered unconditional support with no hesitation or resistance. The business plan evolved and the focus became the training of real estate leaders. There wasn't much in the way of competition and I was confident in my ability to make a difference leadership-wise.

Market research indicated that existing leadership companies were more "institutional." I switched gears and followed in their footsteps, scrapping my original plan. Instead of launching a leadership training program from the platform of A Better Version of You, The Real Estate Leadership Institute was born--and the energy changed immediately. This approach did not work because it was not representative of the real me. I'm organic and approachable, not stuffy and institutional. Trying to be what I thought the business required instead of my genuine self would not have worked long term because authenticity is critical to success. I now acknowledge and appreciate that mine is a fresh approach to leadership that differs in a good way from other training "academies" and "institutes". It was an easy transition back because the business was already in "go" mode. I could make a difference by training my way, but could not make a difference from a perspective that was not the real deal.

Authenticity will attract authentic people into your life. Being your genuine self sends the message that you are trustworthy. True relationships develop where there is trust. I managed real estate offices for most of my career. The most important part of my job in that capacity was to grow the office. I conducted interviews with prospective agents in a fairly predictable manner with the exception of my final litmus test. It was critical that they pass this test or they would not be invited to join our organization.

During the interview I asked myself if this was someone I would have to my home for dinner. Bringing someone home is very different than meeting somewhere for a cup of coffee or having lunch in a restaurant. It created a very personal bond and required trusting my instincts to let them into my life. If the answer was yes, I would share the decision with them and would tell them the selection process that I just mentally went through. "You are someone I would have to my home for dinner." They loved that. On the other hand, if the answer was no, I would not share the reason for the verdict with them. If it was apparent in the interview that they would not be a good fit for the culture of our office, they were not invited to join. It didn't matter if they were consistent producers and would be a benefit to the company's bottom line. I was not willing to risk losing any of my existing valuable associates by adding an unknown factor to the team. You know the saying, one bad apple...

It also made my job much easier. I went to work every day with a team of agents who, down to the last one, would be welcome to my home for dinner. I looked forward to that every day. After hiring in this manner for years, I made good on my promise and invited the staff, agents, and their guests to my home for our annual holiday party. It was a very special evening for all, especially for me.

Trust your instincts. Think of all the things you would miss out on if you were afraid to trust. What if you vowed never to fall in love again after having your heart broken by someone you loved? You might miss out on even greater love a little farther down the road of life. Feel free to put yourself out there. We worry too much about what others think. Let that go! People are so busy living their own lives that they don't have time to pay that much attention to what the rest of us are doing.

In the song "I Am Me," Diana Ross sang, "I can be a better me than anyone can" (1982). I agree and am so glad that I realized how important it was to be my true self and felt confident enough to make a change back to A Better Version of You. Who doesn't want that?

Two

Start at the Core
of the Matter

"Your beliefs become your thoughts, your
thoughts become your words,
Your words become your actions, your
actions become your habits,
Your habits become your values, your
values become your destiny."

— MAHATMA GANDHI

DEFINE YOUR CORE VALUES AND
CLARIFY YOUR "WHY"

The first step toward a self-organized life involves drilling down to our core to identity who we are and why we do what we do. Simon Sinek, the visionary author of *Start with Why*, believes that "finding 'why' is a process of discovery, not invention" (2009). Recognizing the cause or purpose that inspires us to live the life that we do is our "why." In the past it was popular to create a mission statement as a constant reminder to individuals and organizations of who they were, or wanted to be, and what they envisioned when they took the leap of faith to turn their dreams into reality. Mission statements were intended to be more of a description of strategies and culture than the actual spirit or soul. Core values are those principles that form the foundation from which the mission statement operates.

There are numerous values to choose from. It is critical to find the ones that are so important to you, so much your core, that they will continue to define who you are through years of change and evolution. In an ever-changing world, core values are constant. They do not describe the work we do or the strategies we use to reach our goals. Core values inspire our work and how we interact with one another. They are our basic elements. They are practices we use (or should be using) every day in everything we do. They are why we live and breathe, and why we get up in the morning.

It's not a matter of choosing a few words that sound virtuous or right. It's a process that takes time and introspection. Your core values, the essential tenets of who you are, will unfold over time. Just a few simple words will express what you stand for and clearly state why you do the things you do. Be very thoughtful when defining your values. You're not trying to figure out what you want to be when you grow up. You are identifying a few very powerful words to pinpoint the precise values that define you. That means no copying.

Here are a few potent words to get your juices flowing. Read through them to see if any resonate with you:

Accomplished, Accountable, Achieving, Action Oriented, Adventurous, Appreciative, Ardent, Authentic, Balanced, Belief, Beneficent, Benevolent, Candid, Careful, Caring, Creditable, Collaborative, Consistent, Communicative, Community, Competitive, Creative, Daring, Dedicated, Dependable, Determined, Determination, Diversity, Durable, Efficiency, Empowerment, Energetic, Enthusiastic, Ethical, Equality, Excellence, Fairness, Faithful, Family, Fearless, Forgiving, Formidable, Free Thinking, Fresh, Fun, Gallant, Generous, Genuine, Good, Gracious, Grateful, Growth, Happiness, Helpful, Honesty, Honorable, Hope, Imaginative, Influential, Informative, Innovative, Integrity, Intelligence, Joyful, Just, Justice, Kindness, Knowledge, Leadership, Learning, Legacy, Love, Loyalty, Memorable, Merciful, Neighborly, Nimble, Noble, Nonconforming, Nurturing, Obedient, Objective, Open, Open Minded, Opportunity, Optimistic, Organized, Original, Outstanding, Ownership, Passion, Performance, Perseverance, Persistence, Personable, Powerful, Professional, Purity, Quality, Reliability, Respect, Resourceful, Self-Improvement, Serenity, Servant, Sharing, Spirituality,

Strength, Stability, Sturdy, Successful, Teamwork, Togetherness, Tough, Trust, Truth, Unity, Valiant, Vigorous, Virtuous, Wisdom, Yes Minded, Youthful, Zen

It might be easier to start with ten words that are very close to your heart. Through the process of elimination, whittle the ten down to your top five values. You may have chosen several words that are very similar. If that's the case exclude the ones that are the least accurate and keep the few that personify you. This may take a few days. Sleep on the words and what they mean to you. Your own personal core values will become crystal clear in time. When they do, select the two or three that are closest to your core, or to the real, true you.

The next step involves creating a descriptive narrative to bring life to your core values and make them real. Just saying a word doesn't allow you to get your arms around the concept. You can start the process with stream-of-consciousness thinking. Plan to revisit this later to fine-tune your thoughts for clarity. It may require many visits to get it just right. Once you have identified and articulated your personal core values, shout them from the rooftop. Keep a copy in your purse or wallet to review regularly. It's time to start living them every day, in every way.

My personal core values are Authenticity, Balance, and Gratefulness.

Authentic

I am real, genuine, and true to myself. I make decisions with my heart as well as my head, based on my own beliefs and opinions. I live a life that is consistent with my values, not as a passive observer, but with passion for my purpose. I lead a balanced, grounded life and remember where I came from. I am authentically myself, not trying to be anyone else. I earn people's trust by living an authentic life.

Balanced

I live a balanced life. I feel peaceful and grounded when my relationships, career, and accomplishments reflect what is going on in my heart and mind. I challenge myself intellectually on a regular basis, pushing myself to realize my goals, while thoroughly enjoying the ride. I set aside time to reflect and allow my mind to rest. I give and receive love in equal measure. I live well by creating healthy boundaries that provide peace of mind and harmony in my life.

Grateful

I am grateful. I cultivate gratitude and express it daily by counting my many blessings. I focus on the positive. This is healing and life-affirming and keeps my mind-body-spirit healthy, happy, and content. I am thankful for all of the good in my life as well as the challenges, because through them, I am stronger. I am grateful for the many opportunities I have to grow and to learn. I choose to keep my heart open through gratitude regardless of what life brings my way.

Now it's time to carefully consider your own personal core values. The following worksheets will walk you through the process, but please don't feel the need to rush. Really think about the values you will commit to live by, year in and year out, no matter how your life evolves. I have included a list of values and the narratives of my values to aid in your introspection process. If none of these completely embrace the truly unique you, keep digging. This is not one size fits all by any means. With some serious introspection, you will be able to put together those perfect few words that capture your individual essence.

Start by selecting ten core values that will define you now and will remain with you through years of change and evolution.

1.
2.
3.
4.
5.
6.
7.
8.

9.

10.

After considering your top ten, narrow down your selection to the top five.

1.

2.

3.

4.

5.

After thinking it through, further reduce your top five core values to three that will represent the essence of your values.

1.

2.

3.

Now create a descriptive narrative to bring life to your core values and make them real.

1. _____
   _____
   _____
   _____
   _____
   _____

2. _____
   _____
   _____
   _____
   _____
   _____

3. _____
   _____
   _____
   _____
   _____

Congratulations! I know that wasn't easy, but it is critical to moving forward with the next step in your quest for self-organization and self-actualization.

Additional worksheets are available on the website www.abetterversionofyou.com.

Three

Live on Purpose

> "I am here for a purpose and that purpose
> is to grow into a mountain, not to shrink to
> a grain of sand. Henceforth I will apply all
> my efforts to become the highest mountain
> of all and I will strain my potential until it
> cries for mercy."

> — OG MANDINO, AUTHOR OF *THE GREATEST*
> *SALESMAN IN THE WORLD*

Your life's purpose is not just about figuring out who you are and what you do. It's also about figuring out who you do it for. Are you in business for the sole purpose of making money or do you sincerely want to help people live a richer life through your product or service? It isn't necessary to focus on money to make money. Take your influence and contribution to the next level and focus on making a difference and genuinely helping others. Do this and the money will come.

You identified your gifts and talents and committed to your core values in the previous chapter. Now that you have clarified your purpose, combine those strengths and values, and use them for the greater good. Work for a cause that is greater than yourself. In the Bible, Luke 6:38 states, "Give, and it shall be given to you." The universal Law of Tenfold Returns even more generously confirms that whatever you give away—time, labor, love, donations, or anything else—will come back to you multiplied ten times. You will reap what you sow. The very act of giving starts the process. Expressing appreciation for the return you receive completes the cycle. If you truly give from your heart, this works every time.

The best way I know to live on purpose is to serve. It's really quite simple: If you want to be happier, make others happy. If you want to be successful, help others to succeed. Make your purpose in life to give, and not get. The more you delight in giving, the richer your life will be.

For almost four decades, I enjoyed a very successful career in real estate. One of the reasons for my long-term success was that I was never concerned about the amount of commission generated by the transaction. Regardless of whether my clients needed assistance leasing a condominium, or were in the market for a multimillion-dollar home, I served their needs with the same passion and commitment that I felt for every aspect of my business. I listened to their needs and went to work.

My day started at 4:00 a.m. for many years. I did this in an effort to get a head start on the rest of the world. The key to being able to rise so early was having a purpose. If I woke up and couldn't think of anything that I needed or wanted to do, it was very easy to go right back to sleep. That rarely happened. My priorities and goals for the day were clear and written in the evening before bed. I was actually excited to get up and get started because I was doing the small things that needed to be done to reach my bigger goals.

I used those early morning hours proactively. That stolen time was spent attending to the many details that might otherwise have fallen through the cracks—the countless insignificant, but nevertheless important, things that make such a difference in our quality of life. I would put on a pot of coffee, throw in a load of wash, fire up the computer, and give serious thought to the day ahead. What business and personal commitments loomed and what would they require of me? With appliances humming all around me, I was energized and productive. My mind was fresh and without interruptions or distractions, so much could be accomplished. E-mails were sent, files audited, and bills paid. I made sure to make room for grace notes, committing a few minutes writing personal notes to friends, family, clients, and colleagues.

My "power hours" also allowed me to take a walk at first light. This offered a little quiet time to gather my thoughts and set the tone for the day. My best ideas have come to light while walking. There's something about the combination of fresh air, blood pumping, and morning solitude to clarify purpose.

Facebook's Mark Zuckerberg sets a personal challenge for himself every year. He does this to "gain perspective and inspiration for new ideas and products" (2014). Past challenges have included wearing a necktie every day, learning Mandarin, and meeting one new person outside of the company every day. In 2014 he committed to writing at least one "well-considered" thank-you note daily. A handwritten note is a simple gesture that makes a huge difference. Imagine how you feel when you receive a thank-you note. You feel appreciated, valued, and respected. Now imagine how you feel when you send a thank-you note. The effort you put into the writing of the note comes back as a gift, making you feel grateful and gratified. Powerful positive feelings are enjoyed by both the giver and receiver. It's really so easy and it makes such an impact. Zuckerberg sets a great example of living on purpose and making a difference.

I place tremendous importance on sending handwritten notes. I keep boxes of them handy at home, the office, and in my car. Being armed and ready allows me to jot a few notes between appointments, over a cup of coffee, waiting on hold, you name it. It's such a wonderful feeling to see my note on someone's desk or taped to their wall months after they received it. There are so many reasons to write, but you don't really need a reason to reach out to someone with a few heartfelt words. It takes very little effort to make their day, and yours.

As I was writing this chapter, I received a beautiful card with a letter folded inside from a past client, who over many years has become a wonderful friend. His wife was in my book club, and when it was my turn to host the monthly luncheon, I served a very delicious, but very simple-to-make tortilla soup. She went home and suggested they serve that soup at their Italian restaurant. Imagine—tortilla soup on an Italian menu! He took her advice and Martha's Tortilla Soup was added to the weekend offerings. It was a hit, and years later, they still serve it. The purpose of his letter was to thank me for sharing that recipe, along with a few others. It was amazing that he took the time to write such a delightful letter. He definitely made my day.

In 2011 and 2012, I spent time in the hospital recovering from several surgeries. The hospital that treated me mounted whiteboards on the wall opposite the foot of each bed. On them, they listed the names of the staff on each shift, vital statistics, and goals for the day. I loved that. The first few days following surgery, pain management was at the top of the list, but eventually the list grew to include activities like "sit up on the edge of the bed" or "walk three laps around the nurses' station." When I woke up each day and read the list, I was motivated to begin. Unplug me and set me free. Sometimes it took most of the day to meet my goals, but I always did. The staff celebrated each accomplishment with congratulations and high fives as if I had just moved mountains. The daily goals played a big part in my recovery. I could have languished in bed and let nature take its course, but with the encouragement of my caregivers, I stepped up and made every day count.

These days we enjoy a very different morning routine. It's a little kinder, gentler, and certainly less ambitious, but the results are similar. For one thing, my day begins at a more civilized hour. My husband and I enjoy our coffee and the daily newspaper. We compare notes about our intentions for the day and what we must accomplish. There is always a definite purpose. It feels wonderful to wake up with a plan in place to successfully move you closer to your goals and to a better version of you.

Specific

Measurable

Achievable

Realistic

Timely

Four

Set Thoughtful Goals

"Everybody has their own Mount Everest
they were put on this earth to climb."

— Seth Godin, *Linchpin* (2010)

Remember when you were eight years old? When you dreamed, you dreamed big. The sky was the limit. You could be an astronaut, a fireman, a teacher, or in my case, a nun. I was very impressionable when I was eight and the Sisters of Mercy at St. Pius X Catholic School did a thorough job selling their vision. My plan to be a nun was a short-lived dream.

When I was in eighth grade, a representative from Chapman University visited our school to introduce us to World Campus Afloat, known at that time as Semester at Sea. I was quite inspired by the idea of traveling with five hundred students on a voyage around the world while completing a semester of world study courses. I made a decision and set a goal that day to commit one semester of my college adventure to life at sea.

I applied to Chapman in my junior year of high school and was accepted to the land campus in Orange, California. The first week of school found me in the Dean's office asking for acceptance into the Semester at Sea program. It was a small school with strong alumni support. Literally on the spot, I was given a full scholarship for the following spring that would take me around the world in 122 days. There was no paperwork involved. My, how times have changed. Halfway through that semester, I received a letter from the dean asking me to write a note to my benefactors and thank them for the opportunity. I was thrilled to do so and remain forever in their debt.

The impact of that semester was life changing for me. We visited a number of third world countries that would not typically be included on one's travel bucket list. We studied the history, culture, religion, and politics of the countries we visited. I expanded my perspective and by doing so, developed a tremendous respect for what it took to sustain life outside of the United States. My early travels also unleashed an insatiable wanderlust in me, which to this day plays a major part in my life-all because I set a goal.

Set goals that will challenge you to live the life you want to live. As you do this, remember, you cannot go in your life where you haven't gone in your dreams. So dream big! Don't let any self-talk or preconceived ideas hold you back. Do it like you did when you were eight years old. You have very thoughtfully defined your core values and through those values identified your life's purpose, what makes you uniquely you, why you get up in the morning. Take a few minutes to reread those values and set goals that are aligned with them. Consider various areas of your life and make a decision to invest in some wonderful memories, which at the end of the day, is all that really matters. I have identified some segments of life that are important and worthy of cultivating. Please spend a little time absorbing the thought-provoking descriptions and questions for each segment before you set your goals.

- **RELATIONSHIP GOALS**

  Who are the people in your life that you want to maintain or build relationships with? Think about your family and schedule meaningful time with them. It can be something as simple as making the commitment to spend more time with your children or grandchildren. There's no need to make it more difficult by adding qualifying rules, such as limiting it to "quality" time. Just committing to time spent will do the job beautifully. If it's not possible to see them in person, somehow find a way to purposefully include them in your daily life.

  Who are the people who make you feel good when you are around them? Give some thought to building a stronger relationship with them. Identify those positive influences and set goals to include them in your life in a bigger way. While you're at it, identify people at the other end of the spectrum who don't bring out the best in you, or who drain your resources, mentally or physically. Make a determined effort to move away from those people.

I had some clients who were an absolute drain on me and offered nothing in return for my efforts. They owned a number of homes and were constantly looking to me for market updates and professional advice regarding property values and holding-versus-selling strategies. They stalked my open houses, monopolizing my time. They were the ones with critical time-sensitive questions or crises every time I tried to take a few days off. Nothing could wait. I never did any real business with them, serving more as a real estate ATM that was set up for withdrawals only.

I made the decision to somehow gracefully back away from their constant neediness. I was working on how I would accomplish this without hurting any feelings when I noticed one of their properties was on the market for sale. It was listed with someone from out of town at a price that I had recently recommended to them. They were using me to orchestrate their every move with no intention of hiring me to do the job. Problem solved. Once they were listed with someone else, I couldn't ethically discuss real estate with them. It was easy from that point on to recommend that they speak to their agent about their real estate needs.

If you have outgrown your friends, it may be time to foster new ones. Jim Rohn, one of the world's foremost business philosophers encourages "You must constantly ask yourself these questions: Who am I around? What are they doing to me? What have they got me reading? What have they got me saying? Where do they have me going? What do they have me thinking? And, most important, what do they have me becoming? Then ask yourself they big question: Is that okay?" (1994). Choose carefully. The people closest to us greatly affect our attitude, motivation, and decisions. Make a goal to surround yourself with positive people who are dedicated to your success, and you to theirs.

Now think about professional relationships that you need to strengthen. Find and invest in networking opportunities to broaden your horizons. Use the same process for networking in business that you use to develop personal relationships. Network with intention by purposely scheduling time on a regular basis. All relationships will grow and strengthen when you show a sincere interest in them.

- **PHYSICAL GOALS**
  Give serious thought to how you want to look and feel on a daily basis. If you have been trying to turn your body into something that it isn't, set a more

reasonable goal. Oprah Winfrey, with her unlimited resources and access to self-improvement gurus (cooks, personal trainers, etc.), can't maintain her weight when she tries to be too thin. Take a page from her playbook. Aim for healthy, which may not be thin. Acknowledge and accept that we are all built differently. You will experience more success in this area if you honor your true body type and set realistic goals.

It might be time to rethink your wardrobe or hairstyle. If you have become very casual in your manner of dress, you may want to step up your game by dressing up a little more. On the other hand, if you are accustomed to a very corporate environment, it might be time to relax a little.

Daily exercise is critical even if it comes in small doses. Exercise is excellent for peace of mind, it reduces stress and anxiety, and is generally good for our soles and our soul.

- **SPIRITUAL GOALS**
Spirituality can mean many things to many people. Belief in a higher power is vital, in my opinion, and that higher power can manifest itself in different ways. There are numerous traditions and philosophies to choose from; however, spirituality begins with the practice of anything that nourishes your heart, mind, or soul. Consider prayer and meditation

as well as a solitary hike, enjoying a period of silence, or gratitude and thanksgiving of the moment you are living. Clarify what your faith means to you, honor it, and incorporate it into your life. Profound value can be derived from confirming your purpose on this earth.

Practice self-love. Acceptance of your faults and imperfections, and appreciation for all that is good should be acknowledged and recognized in this area of your life.

Count your blessings and focus on the positive. Live with hope in your heart. If you get your mind focused on the good, your spirit will be right behind. I'm convinced that no matter how much is wrong, more is right. Commit to concentrating on the right. Find ways to remind yourself of the good in your life every chance you get.

- **FINANCIAL GOALS**
Where do you want to be at the end of the month financially? The end of the year? At retirement? I am surprised and disappointed in the number of people I know who make an excellent living and spend every penny before they make it. Have financial goals and be fiscally responsible. "More, more, I'm still not satisfied" is a common, but very unsatisfying way to live. My mother taught us growing up that our mortgage or rent should

never exceed 30 percent of our income. That continues to be a prudent rule of thumb today. You won't find a silver bullet to success when it comes to financial goals. In a nutshell, your income must be greater than your expenses. It's just that easy. You can back into financial goals by starting with a budget. Housing, cars, food, medical, insurance, and so forth are all givens. Don't forget to budget for life's emergencies, gifts, continuing education, and self-improvement.

Eliminate all nonessential expenses first. As you set goals in this area, be very realistic with yourself. Look at your fixed expenditures and disposable income. Maybe a helpful goal would be to stop eating out. This would undoubtedly result in a healthier physical you as well as a healthier fiscal you.

When setting financial goals, you can't go wrong by taking the advice of George S. Clason in *The Richest Man in Babylon*. He recommends setting aside 10 percent of your income regularly. If you haven't read the book you should, and if you have, this might be a good time to reread it and start planning for your future today. If 10 percent is too much, start with something less and save it consistently until you build the saving habit and break the spending mold. Don't underestimate the power of compounding interest when it comes to savings. Even a small amount saved consistently can become significant over time.

Now revisit your hopes-and-dreams list and start allocating funds toward those. I will talk more about planning for retirement in chapter 14. Start thinking about that now no matter how old you are. It will come fast. Be honest and put some goals in place that will set you up for a life that offers peace of mind in your golden years.

- **PROFESSIONAL/CAREER GOALS**

   Does your career currently energize and fulfill you? If not, your goal might be to find a new path. Do a little self-assessment. What makes your soul happy and your heart sing? What do you get so into that time flies by? Is it possible to navigate in that direction? If so, what steps must you take to get where you want to go?

   If your assessment confirms that you are in the right place, ask yourself where you go from here and what steps you need to take to make that happen. Raise the bar income-wise or production-wise.

   Regardless of where you are professionally, it is always advisable to update your skills and your résumé. Set some goals to take classes, obtain a designation, or take on more responsibility. Determine what it will take to get to the next level and make sure the people who can help you get there are aware of your intentions.

- **RECREATION/HOBBY GOALS**

  It's time to get out and play. Remember the old adage "All work and no play makes Jack a dull boy"? It's true. How you play is totally up to you. Find your passion. It makes you more interesting and so much happier. Some people like sports and interacting with friends in their spare time. Others like to curl up quietly with a book. As long as you are partaking in an activity that is legal, ethical, relatively safe, and gives you pleasure, go for it! There are many activities to choose from, so definitely choose at least one. If you select an activity that involves other participants, you will be supporting your goal to network and (re)build relationships.

  To avoid feeling overwhelmed, schedule recreational breaks to relieve stress and recharge your batteries. Keep a pair of tennis shoes handy. When I was on overload or stuck in place, I would throw on my walking shoes and take a one-mile, fifteen-minute walk around our local lake. I was back at my desk within twenty-five minutes and energized to push through whatever had been stopping me. It can be that easy.

  If going out to play sounds like unproductive time and you feel the need to have more of a purpose in your downtime, hobbies are for you. Think back to your childhood for inspiration. What did you enjoy doing so much that you lost track of time?

Explore new avenues for growth and learning and build some goals around it.

- **GIVEBACK/LEGACY GOALS**

  How do you want to be remembered? How do you want people to describe your life and your contribution to the world? For most of us, this has more to do with building lasting memories than negotiating world peace, curing cancer, or changing the world as we know it. If you have a special talent or passion, consider mentoring someone as a way to pay it forward. Spend time with the people you love now, so that later in life, they will cherish that time with you and reminisce about it.

  Find a charity that reflects your values and/or supports a cause that is near and dear to your heart. If you can spare the money, donate to the cause. If you cannot give money, give the gift of time.

  Giving back on a daily basis doesn't necessarily need to be about money. Make a goal to smile at everyone you see. They will smile back and, hopefully, smile at the next person they see; it's wonderfully contagious. Or commit to giving a sincere compliment to at least one person every day. It will not only make their day, but it carries the added benefit of making your day, too. Be generous. Spreading joy costs nothing and comes back to you in spades. Goals as simple as this will leave a lasting legacy.

Now I imagine that after reading this chapter you feel a little overwhelmed. I have to admit that I felt overwhelmed writing it. Set yourself up for success by picking one area to work on first. Make a goal in that area and commit to a plan by breaking it down into systems that will enable you to achieve that goal. Once you have that area under control, choose another one and work on that. Picture the juggler who entertains by spinning a number of plates in the air. He starts with one. When it is spinning effortlessly, he adds one more. As he gets the second one up and running, he checks on the first one and gives it a little push, if needed. And so on. If he tried to spin them all at once, he would fail, just as we would if we tried to get all areas of our life spinning seamlessly at the same time. Start with one.

What part of your life will you focus on first? Select from this list of possible goal categories and begin to transform your life for good.

1. Relationship Goals
2. Physical Goals
3. Spiritual Goals
4. Financial Goals
5. Professional/Career Goals
6. Recreation/Hobby Goals
7. Giveback/Legacy Goals

Once the goal category has been selected, further break down your objectives. If one of your goals is to work on your relationships, you may want a weekly date night or an hour a week of one-on-one with your children.

Please select your goal category and your specific goals within that category:

Goal Category:
Objective:

Goal Category:
Objective:

Goal Category:
Objective:

Remember: Start with just a limited number of goal categories so you can retain focus.

~~Impossible~~

~~Unable~~

~~Unsolvable~~

~~Undoable~~

Five

Embrace the Art of Prioritizing

"The key is not to prioritize what's on your schedule, but to schedule your priorities."

— STEPHEN COVEY, THE SEVEN HABITS OF HIGHLY EFFECTIVE PEOPLE (1989)

The most important use of your time is spent doing things that move you closer to your goals. Doug Firebaugh, president of the Home Business Radio Network, urges, "Every day do something that will inch you closer to a better tomorrow". We are all pulled in too many different directions with too much to do, and not enough time to do it. The only way to get the vital things done is by prioritizing the importance of each item and managing the time you spend on individual tasks. Setting goals and meeting deadlines creates the framework for successful self-organization. How do you eat an elephant? One bite at a time. That's the same way you achieve big goals. Break them down into small bites and concentrate on first things first.

Hopefully, you have identified goals relevant to several areas of your life suggested in chapter 4, such as business, relationships, and finances. Once your goals are in place, commit to making consistent progress on a daily basis. It is essential to also allocate quality time to work on yourself. This will avoid the feeling of resentment that comes over you when you spend all of your time living for others with no time dedicated to replenishing your own body, mind, and spirit.

Now it's time to devote your energy to the things that will make a difference. Always ask yourself the question, "Is what I am doing right now moving me closer to or further from my goal?" Devote your time to the things that matter. It's not about working faster. It's about spending your time on the right things. If you have lost touch with what is essential, take some time to revisit and clarify your objectives and purpose. It's very easy to get distracted and off course. When this happens, ask yourself the following critical self-organizational questions:

- **Does what I am doing contribute to the goal?**
  It's easy to confuse being busy with being productive. One of my clients was a high-powered executive and never let me forget it. I represented him many times during my career as he bought and sold homes. When we were involved in a transaction, we met frequently to update him on the progress

I was making on his behalf. We would review the list of what had transpired since our last meeting. Regardless of how much work this represented on my part, if his home hadn't sold or he hadn't found the perfect property to purchase, I could count on hearing, "Don't mistake activity for results."

In my business, I set goals that clearly spelled out the number of homes I would sell and how I would do it. They were itemized by the number of sales representing buyers and the number where I was the seller's agent. Having been caught on the wrong side of the market with too many listings that weren't selling or too many buyers facing very low inventory, I learned that it is necessary to maintain a balance between the two. It didn't take me long to realize that time spent with prospects who would not prequalify through a lender or demonstrate proof of funds were "lookers" and not "buyers." It was a waste of time to show them homes when they were not motivated to buy. My work would not result in a home purchase, therefore, time spent on their behalf would not bring me closer to my goal. I moved on.

- **Should I be increasing/decreasing time spent in this area?**
  The answer is simple. If you want to be successful, spend less time on busy work and more time prospecting. Implementing this is the hard part. When I was building my real estate career, I was

told that specializing in, or "farming," a neighbor-hood was the most efficient way to build a long-term, successful business. I take direction well and so I started to prepare to farm my neighborhood. I spent a long time getting ready to get started. When I did finally commit, my business took off just as I was told it would. I made the decision to increase the time I spent doing this and added another neighborhood, and then another, until my time was quite consumed by getting my face in front of the homeowners, in person or by mail. I planned neighborhood events which took even more time, but proved to be very much worth the effort in the long run.

- **Can someone else perform this task?**
  Now that I was experiencing more success, my files needed attention. Paperwork is not my strong suit, and clearly not the best use of my time. I made a great decision and hired someone to handle my escrow transactions and listing follow-up. It's always best to play to your strengths. Not only will you do a better job when you flex a talent muscle, but you will also enjoy the process so much more. Your job satisfaction will shine through. People prefer to work with people who have passion for what they do. So concentrate on doing what you do best and hire someone to do the rest.

- **Should I say "no" to this?**

  The sooner you can learn the fine art of saying "no," the happier you will be. I have to admit that I had a need to be supermom. I was room mom, team mom, cookie-baking mom, and party-planning mom. It simply got to be too much. As my career took off, I stopped enjoying it, but still could not manage to say "no." The requests continued. I practiced saying "no," but it always came out "yes." I'm not sure how I got the courage, but one day when I was called on to contribute three dozen cookies for a school event, I said that I wouldn't be able to contribute the actual cookies, but I would be glad to contribute money to the cause. As it turned out, no one needed me to spread myself too thin; they simply needed cookies.

- **Can I substitute this activity for something else on my schedule?**

  How many items can you layer into your daily schedule before something slips through the cracks? Or before you crack? It's imperative to identify and eliminate whatever isn't moving you closer to your goals. If you begin to feel pulled in too many directions, take a look at your agenda and find a way to lighten the load. When you decide that something is not a priority, drop it from your schedule as soon as you can gracefully do so. It's important to be a contributor and take your turn hosting groups or chairing events, but one event or season might be enough. If you have done your part, turn over the reins to someone else, at least for the time being. When your time is booked to capacity and a new activity demands attention, make a decision to let something go.

- **Do I need to create a system around this?**
  Creating systems is the very best way to get a lot done in the shortest amount of time, with the least frustration to you. In the beginning, I juggled a few clients at a time. I would call them, or they would call me, at random times for updates. As my business grew, this became challenging. All of a sudden, I had too many names and details to remember, and risked being caught off guard. Some clients were needier than others, and without realizing it, I would spend all of my time on one demanding client at the expense of the others. To solve the problem, I developed a communication system. At our first meeting, I set my clients' expectations about how and when we would connect. My system for communicating meant that whatever was done for one, was done for all. I called every client on Monday to update them regarding recent marketing, the results of that marketing, and feedback or level of interest from prospects. I also used that phone call to suggest a price adjustment if the market wasn't responding to their

current price. I discussed their position in the marketplace and explained that agents usually showed only a few homes in each neighborhood and that we needed to be priced properly to make the cut. They were typically reluctant to agree to a price reduction in the first few rounds, but after weeks of asking and weeks of sitting on the market, they saw the value in improving their price.

In addition to the phone call, a weekly Multiple Listing report detailing recent sales and current competition was sent to them. This often led to a call from a seller asking me to price their home below the competition so that they would be positioned properly to be the next home sold.

Systems are critical to the organizational success in every area of your life and will allow you time to breathe. I have systems in place for laundry, grocery shopping, meals, gift giving, card sending, and so on. You will read more on the importance of systems in chapter 7.

Prioritizing helps us make choices about how to spend our time. The 80/20 Rule is all about prioritizing. It contends that 80 percent of our daily activities contribute only 20 percent to the value of our work. So by concentrating on only the most important tasks, you will still realize most of the value. Focus your efforts on the most important activities and you will not only achieve more, but you will also have more time and energy to pursue other interests.

Which tasks should we do and which tasks should we let go or delegate? The first step requires a list of tasks and schedules and some thought to prioritize each item in order of importance. What combination of urgent/important/not urgent/not important is it?

A. If it's very important and/or urgent, assign it to the A group. Completing the high priority A and B tasks contributes significantly to your long-term success. Both are important, but A tasks require immediate attention. Focusing on these tasks first will also keep things moving in the right direction and keep you out of trouble by avoiding a crisis.

B. If it's important, but not urgent, it can be relegated to the B group. You should be spending most of your time on this group. Because these tasks are not urgent, there are no looming deadlines and typically no stress. Your B group will offer the most rewards in the long run. Self-improvement, education, honing your skills, and spending time with family are all B tasks. A day spent doing B work is, indeed, a good day.

C. The C group is comprised of anything that is on your list that is neither urgent nor important. These are the "I'll get to it when I get to it" things and it's OK if they don't get done today...or ever.

Practicing good stewardship should be a priority. Being a good steward means you take care of what you own. Many people have developed an attitude that everything we own is disposable. When market values were going up, a number of people in my area purchased new, very expensive homes that they couldn't afford. They had the wherewithal to get their foot in the door, but not enough to upgrade and maintain the property appropriately. They bought the home with the idea that they would sell it at a profit before anything needed to be done. Sometimes the market didn't cooperate and they weren't able to make the profit they hoped for, or recoup their money for that matter. So they stayed awhile. When I was called in to list the property for sale, I was often shocked by the condition. I have been expected to market multimillion-dollar homes with lightbulbs burned out and pet-stained yards—in short, sad and neglected homes.

The same philosophy should apply to cars, clothing, and the like. Taking care of our possessions should be a priority. It does take time and effort to keep things maintained. Instead of buying new every time (especially when you don't have the money), make a plan to stay on top of what you own. It takes work, yes, but is so important because it demonstrates pride. My mother, at ninety-one, found a hole in her sock and asked me if I had a darning needle and some thread. That's generational stewardship at its best. I did not have darning supplies because that's going a bit far even for me, but you get the point. Make it a priority to be a good steward of what you own.

It takes considerable effort to stay focused and stick to your priorities. I have to confess that I did not maximize my time, energy, or effort today. Wasting time is a pet peeve of mine and failing to complete projects is draining. My primary objective today was to write about prioritizing. It has taken me most of the day to complete my task because I have allowed and/or invented so many interruptions. I will give myself points for finishing, even if it wasn't in the most expedient manner. Tomorrow I will try again. After all, practice makes perfect.

At the end of a focused day, you will feel relaxed, accomplished, and in position for another successful tomorrow. Success breeds success. You will not feel stressed or anxious about what you didn't get done, because concentrating on the things that are important to you moves you closer to your goals and to the life you have imagined—a better version of you.

Six

~~Eliminate~~ Reduce
Procrastination

"Habitual procrastinators will readily
testify to all the lost opportunities, missed
deadlines, failed relationships, and even
monetary losses incurred just because of
one nasty habit of putting things off until it
is often too late."

— STEPHEN RICHARDS, *OVERCOMING
PROCRASTINATION* (2012)

The best way to get unstuck is to confront the real reason you avoid putting off what eventually must be
done. Take the time to think through what exactly is holding you back. The only way to do this is to have a realistic
understanding of why we do it in the first place.

What causes us to procrastinate? We are human. We
are easily distracted and allow various and sundry things to

derail us from our pathway to success. Here are a few real-life side-trackers that may be causing you to drag your feet:

- **Lack of discipline**
  You may be stuck for a reason you can't quite put your finger on. Here are a few ideas that might help you get disciplined and moving forward:
  - Reach out to an accountability partner or hire a coach to professionally guide you.
  - Identify mentors and others you can trust to ask the right questions to get you going in the right direction. Offer to assist them in the same way. The buddy system is alive and well. Working in conjunction with another person makes us accountable and gets us back in action.
  - Set a deadline. Assign a consequence if you don't get the job done or a reward if you accomplish it in a timely manner.
  - Read a few pages of something motivating before you begin. It might be just the jump start you need.
  - Stop your project on a high note so that you are excited to get back to it. For example, I try to quilt at least a few minutes every day. I never stop when the sewing machine needs rethreading or the bobbin runs out. That would require time spent doing a mundane chore before I begin again. I always make sure everything is set to go and I'm on the cusp of something fun before

stopping a session. With a little planning, I look forward to getting back to it as soon as possible.

We all struggle from time to time. Find a fun approach that piques your interest and get going as soon as you can. Making visible progress is an excellent motivator.

- **Not seeing the task as your job**
  You can't manage every task and be solely responsible for every decision. If you feel that the task could be handled by someone other than yourself, delegate it. When you delegate something, be very clear about the outcome you are looking for, but not about the methodology. There is no need to clone yourself to get the job done correctly and in a timely manner. Communicate the outcome you would like to see: "Here is where things are today. Here is where they need to be." Now stand back and let them get the job done, their way. You will save time and energy which will free you up to focus on your priorities and accomplish those things that will provide the biggest benefit.

- **Feeling incompetent to complete the task**
  If you feel incompetent or unqualified, educate yourself. Everything is available at our fingertips, literally. You can research online, sign up for webinars, take a class, or invest in a few books. Feeling

prepared and capable can make all the difference. If, after researching your options, you still feel out of your league, enlist help. Look for solutions as soon as you recognize the need. That will start things moving again, with renewed energy.

- **Feeling overwhelmed**
  If you feel overwhelmed or that the task is insurmountable, break it down into smaller pieces. Chip away at each segment until the task feels manageable and you are able to complete it. Try motivating yourself with very small goals. As you reach your first benchmark, you are inspired to accomplish more. Keep it simple.

  It's draining to surround yourself with unfinished projects. Pick one job, finish it, and check it off your list. How do you feel? Energized, right? Now use that energy to move on to the next project, complete it, and go to the next. Be sure to celebrate each small victory until you feel you have won the day. Tomorrow you will feel as if you have a head start and you can hit the ground running. It's all about the mind-set.

- **Fear of making a mistake**
  In the words of the late Robert H. Schuller, Christian televangelist and motivational speaker, "What great thing would you attempt if you knew you could not fail?" Fear of making a mistake can paralyze you.

Before you let that happen, ask for help. Get a second opinion and a second set of hands or eyes on the job. Then move forward with confidence. Ask yourself what the worst outcome would be if you were to make a mistake. Consider post-it notes. Those handy little sticky notes came about when Dr. Spencer Silver, a scientist at 3M, was trying to develop a super-strong adhesive. Instead, he "accidentally created a low-tack, reusable, pressure-sensitive adhesive" (1968). That was a happy mistake that ended up working out in a very big way. Think serendipity, take a chance, and get moving.

- **Interruptions and distractions**
Focus. Stop inviting/creating interruptions. Set a time limit to work on your task. Focus only on that during the time that you set. Since I sat down to write this, I have lost my focus a number of times. I have made and received several personal phone calls and texts, booked a hotel reservation online, and while I was there, surfed the net for a new recipe for dinner. From there, it was just too easy to connect with a few friends on Facebook and check my e-mail again. Then I cleaned out my wallet. I know. I noticed that it was a mess when I removed my credit card to book the hotel. I wish I was making this up.

Try to work in an interruption-free zone. Coworkers will respect your wishes if you let them know that you need quiet for X amount of time. For those of you who work at home, this is more difficult. It might help to keep regular office hours or set up some boundaries to represent the time that you are unavailable. I worked out of my home office for a while and understand that not everyone acknowledges the importance of a distraction-free environment. Neighbors dropped in randomly and the kids always had something urgent to share with me the moment I got on the phone. It's up to you set clear rules.

- **Eat a frog first thing in the morning**
I imagine you have heard this phrase, or some version of it, many times. Get the toughest job out of the way as soon as you can. It will energize and inspire you to accomplish so much more. As a Realtor, I often had to deliver disappointing news to my clients. The longer I put it off, the worse I felt about it. I tried everything in my power to fix the situation before conveying bad news. What I finally understood was that it was their news, not mine. Loans denied, buyers backing out, or whatever went wrong was usually out of my control. My clients deserved to know immediately. I learned to make the call, give them an update, and offer a few possible solutions to the problem. As the principal, it was their problem. As the agent, it was my job to lay out the options and represent them in their decision. Many times a loan that has been denied can be repackaged and

resubmitted for approval. Buyers threaten to cancel, but through the art of negotiation (think credit or concession), they are back in the game. When you eat the frog, you empower yourself to face whatever the rest of the day may bring.

- **Indulging in crisis management**
Some people can't get unstuck until crisis is upon them. It takes rising panic to shake things up. They may crave the adrenaline rush of pending disaster or the feeling of self-importance produced by always being in the eye of the storm. If control is the goal, acknowledge that some things will always be out of your control and concentrate on the power that you do have. Managing your life by crisis is ineffective and exhausting, and will ultimately hold you back. Nothing beats a deep breath, clarity of the situation, and one foot in front of the other.

- **Lack of self-organization**
Learning self-organization is definitely a work in progress. Think through a typical day. What are the things that steal precious minutes on a regular basis? One day I was looking up some information on the Internet that would help me with a project I was working on. The next thing I knew, I was watching a video about how to effortlessly remove the seeds from a pomegranate. That's a true story and it was, admittedly, a very interesting video. I have no idea

how I ended up there, but I do know that valuable time was wasted, unless some day I need to remove the seeds from a pomegranate.

I have used the example many times about timing phone calls. When I was very busy, I would make or receive about sixty calls a day. If each conversation lasted one minute, that represented one hour of my workday. Those same calls stretching out to three minutes would eat up an additional two hours of my day. I find that alarming. Make your minutes count. They add up to hours in no time at all.

Keep reading. This book is filled with many opportunities for self-organization. Small adjustments on a daily basis will get you to a better version of you.

If you can relate to any of the difficulties listed above, you are not alone. We all procrastinate to one degree or another. Once you have identified the problem(s), make a decision about simple systems you will put into place to solve the problem. Challenge yourself to take the action that will help you get unstuck and move you closer to your goals—starting now.

S aves

Y ou

S tress

T ime

E nergy

M oney

Seven

Put Simple Systems in Place

"Life is really simple, but we insist on
making it complicated."

— CONFUCIUS

We can become overwhelmed with our list of goals, especially if, like most people, we try to change everything at once. That's exactly why most New Year's resolutions fail. We try to do too much, too soon. Are your goals so big that you don't know where or how to begin? Do you wonder when you will find the time to work on them? Single out one small goal and build a system around it. Ease into it by starting with something manageable.

I used to make a big deal out of filing my income taxes. The truth is, I was unprepared, dreaded the process, and procrastinated to the point of absurdity. One day I decided that the drama was unnecessary and put a few systems in place to make it easier to file when the deadline loomed.

Here's what prompted the systems. The IRS paid me an unexpected visit and the first thing the auditor focused on was the total of all bank deposits. He asked me to explain why more money passed through my account than was claimed as income. My response was that I occasionally loaned money to friends with the understanding that they would repay the debt whenever they had money to spare. It usually came back in small amounts that were deposited into my account upon receipt. Because one sum went out and a number of smaller amounts came back (sometimes over several tax years), it was difficult to reconcile the figures and impossible to dredge up the details and dates from memory. I was naive enough to think a simple explanation on my part would suffice. It did not. Hence, the need for a system to track deposits.

This system involved sending a copy of every check to my CPA before it was deposited into my bank account. He saved those copies in my file all year so that we could easily reconstruct the income side of the equation. Another system was to fax or scan my credit card statement to him at the end of every month so that he could categorize the expenses one month at a time. When the deadline approached in April, I had a sufficient head start and was in position to file in a timely manner, sans the agony. A few minutes spent each month saved hours of angst at the eleventh hour.

My desk had a large file drawer which served as my receipts "system." That term is used loosely because, admittedly, it was a lousy system. I placed every receipt in the drawer, face up in a pile. When I met my husband, John, I was delighted to learn that he actually enjoyed maintaining organized files, a task that is clearly not my forte. When he saw the drawer of receipts, he sighed, "Oh, my. Well, at least everything is in chronological order." Of course they weren't, but hope springs eternal. When something was needed from the drawer, I simply fished around until the document was found. It was later "refiled" in the drawer on top of the stack. I have happily relinquished responsibility in this arena, and all parties, including my husband, CPA, and the IRS, are grateful.

You've heard the saying "An apple a day keeps the doctor away." We can all agree that eating an apple every day constitutes a healthy habit. But here's where things go wrong. We forget to eat the apple on Monday and Tuesday. By Wednesday we feel that it's too late in the week to make a difference, so we adjust our plan and decide to eat all of the apples on Saturday, "when we have more time." Recognizing that eating all of the apples at once would have a decidedly unhealthy effect on us, we elect to do nothing. And there we are. Start with something manageable, a slice of apple a day.

I used this example with real estate agents whose business plans included specializing in a specific geographic area. The agents were typically overzealous in the beginning and would take on too many homes. Overwhelmed, they were never able to carve out the necessary time to meet their ambitious goals. Days went by. By midweek, when they still had not been out to prospect, they would announce that they were going to blitz the whole neighborhood on Saturday "when more people would be home." Saturday came and went because something would always get in the way of a full day of prospecting.

Start small and grow into the commitment. Keep it simple. A small commitment requires less willpower and is far less intimidating. Build confidence and a strong foundation by cuing yourself up for success rather than failure. Doing that one small thing every single day reinforces the habit and supports your goals.

When I was a novice Realtor, my game plan included knocking on ten doors as a daily minimum. I could knock on more, which was possible most days, but my commitment was to no fewer than ten per day. Ten was a manageable number in spite of the weather, uncomfortable shoes, or lack of time. No excuses. In the beginning this was a daily to-do and, eventually, it became a routine practice that served me very well.

If you want to reconnect with your clients, set up a system that requires you to consistently send even one note, make one call, or meet with one person from your client list. It's OK to do more, but never less. I put a system in place one year in October, committing to contacting three past clients per day. I was not looking forward to it because I felt guilty about not having stayed in touch with them. The first week I called the easy ones. The people I had crossed paths with occasionally, who weren't completely out of the loop. We chatted about their family, career, and home. The following weeks should have been more difficult because they were people I truly had lost contact with, but something wonderful happened. Everyone was happy to hear from me. No one acted as if they should have heard from me sooner. This project resulted in more invitations to holiday parties, happy hours, and family dinners than one could ever imagine. The following year, my production tripled. It can be that simple.

Give some thought to areas in your life that hold you back. When you identify one, consider the steps you take when completing the task or project. Once you break down the process, try to identify a few steps that can be eliminated. For example, if bill paying is your worst nightmare write down the steps necessary to write the check, address the envelope, find and adhere the stamps, and mail them. Now think about how few steps are needed to set up online bill pay. Streamlining the process will make it more palatable and help you work through it quicker. Try to create a system or strategy that is so simple that it cannot fail. Then muster up a little willpower. In order for your system to work, it must become a habit and willpower is an essential ingredient for the first few months until the habit takes hold. Consistency is crucial to making this work over the long term.

I have a friend who is a life coach. She loves the coaching sessions, but does not like setting up her appointments. To schedule a session, you call the phone number on her card and leave a message. A day or two later, she calls back and leaves a message with a few available time slots. You call her back and leave a message with your selection and, hopefully, she calls you back at some point to confirm the time. It's no wonder she doesn't like to schedule. She has created an overly cumbersome process. A simple solution might be a website where clients can e-mail a request for an appointment. The e-mail might include a short form where the prospect can indicate time preferences and availability. One response should set the appointment. It would help to include a questionnaire on the website for a first-time client to submit prior to the meeting. This would speed up the "getting to know you" process at the inaugural meeting. Together you could move right into the "here's how I can help" phase of the session. That's a much better use of valuable time and a seemingly user-friendly system.

A few years ago I decided to share my cancer journey. A blog seemed to be the best method of communication, but blogging required new skills as well as new strategies and consistent daily and weekly procedures. I began by posting three times per week and then slowed down to twice weekly. I would select a topic and make a few notes on day one. The following day I would write the post and sleep on it overnight. I polished it up one last time before posting and then started working on my next topic. In this way, it became a simple, manageable system instead of one more thing to do in an already-busy day.

Consider the power of lists as simple systems. Steve Mariboli, speaker and author of *Life, the Truth, and Being*

Free, says, "Re-name your 'To-Do' list your 'Opportunities' list. Each day is a treasure chest filled with limitless opportunities: take joy in checking many off your list" (2009). Lists become the critical first step to successful prioritizing. We live in an era of constant information overload. It feels as if the floodgates are always open. It's almost impossible to deal with it effectively. You're fighting a losing battle if you try to keep it all straight without a list.

One of the best books I have read in recent years is *The Checklist Manifesto* (2010) by Atul Gawande. The book is not about your average daily to-do list. It's about utilizing brief strategic lists to perform the same tasks over and over. Gawande profiles many applications in various industries, but the most recognizable is the airline pilot's checklist, which is completed prior to each and every flight. It might seem excessive to require a pilot to go through a comprehensive checklist procedure when he or she has completed hundreds of successful flights. The truth is, the reason the pilot has made so many successful flights is that he or she started with a checklist. When something becomes rote, it is easier to skip a step without realizing it. In the case of airplanes, one minor omission can become a death sentence.

Atul Gawande is a surgeon. He made tremendous strides in the operating room at Johns Hopkins Hospital by creating lists to avoid the spread of infection. He started by designing a checklist that focused on just one of the hundreds of daily tasks that intensive-care-unit teams handle daily—inserting a pic line. The list is so simple that it seems unnecessary.

Doctors are supposed to: (1) wash their hands with soap, (2) clean the patient's skin with chlorhexidine antiseptic, (3) put sterile drapes over the entire patient, (4) wear a mask, hat, sterile gown, and gloves, and (5) put a sterile dressing over the insertion site once the line is in.

It seems so simple, but the results showed that over one-third of the time, doctors skipped at least one step. Once the list was being followed religiously, the infection rate dropped dramatically. Johns Hopkins Hospital calculated that in one year, use of the list prevented "forty-three infections and eight deaths and saved two million dollars." Lists are simple, but powerful, systems.

In my younger years, I was able to retain an amazing amount of facts and figures in my head, including all of my clients' phone numbers. The numbers were committed to memory until the transaction closed and then they were quickly forgotten. I never missed birthdays or holidays and rarely forgot an item that was needed at the grocery store. Even back then, when my memory was sharp, lists were critical to keeping my life in balance. I have always been such a dedicated list maker that when something is completed that is not on my list, it is quickly added, just for the satisfaction of crossing it off.

As a Realtor, I used lists as systems to track every aspect of my business. I held open houses on most weekends for more than three decades. Open houses required a very thorough list to ensure that I was as prepared as possible to sell the home. In today's world, it doesn't take as much preparation prior to the event. We are able to access all of the Multiple Listing information on our mobile devices, as needed. However, for most of my career, if I didn't look up recent sales and current competition before setting up shop, there was a good chance someone would ask a question that I could not answer. At some point, I grew lax about using the list and left myself open to the risk of showing up without all of the tools needed to do a proper job. Lists are easy to use, but some days easier than others. Cutting corners can be costly.

When I listed a home for sale, my system consisted of a simple, but cast-in-stone, checklist. It included all of the vital tasks such as completing contracts and disclosures, installing a sign and lockbox, writing ads, and scheduling a photographer. That was the easy part. The list became more important to the process as the marketing time lengthened. It called for follow-up, including requesting and forwarding comments from Realtors and prospects, providing weekly updates regarding changes in the market, and discussing price adjustments. My follow-up was the factor that differentiated me from my competition. The sellers and I worked as a team, and even if their home didn't sell, they knew that I was steadfast in my dedication to getting the job done. With this type of personal service, I was able to maintain a positive relationship with my clients, relist the property if the contract expired, and count on testimonials and referrals to their family and friends.

Here's a system that was not in place, but was definitely needed. As an agent, I consistently managed an average of approximately a dozen listings. Every month I listed a few houses, sold a few houses, and was disappointed to see one or two expire along the way. I was never able to get a handle on the timing of my expiring listings. The Multiple Listing Service would update at midnight and by 9:00 a.m., my clients would have received about twenty phone calls from agents claiming to possess the secret ingredient necessary to sell their home—an ingredient that, according to them, I apparently lacked.

My husband, John, shared this very easy system for managing expiring listings. At the initial meeting, he and the sellers would discuss the length of the contract. It usually involved a six-month commitment. John would tell them that he was going to schedule the expiration date on the last day of the month. If he listed the home on January 20 for a period of six months, the expiration date would be July 31. The clients were content, he had a few additional days to get the home sold, and he only thought about expiring listings once a month. On the last day of each month, he reviewed his contracts. If something was expiring, he contacted the sellers to execute paperwork to extend the listing. If he, or they, had no interest in continuing, he would communicate with them regarding picking up the sign and lockbox and returning their key. Genius. Just one more reason why I wish we had met earlier.

Finally, here's an example of a system that fails, without fail, when I get careless. I enjoy cooking and trying new recipes which are usually a success the first time around. Following the instructions exactly as they are written ensures that the dish will come out looking like the appealing picture. When the dish is less than stellar, it's usually a recipe that I have made several times. The tendency is to get complacent, take shortcuts, or simply overlook a step. It's not life threatening, but certainly disappointing. Success is ensured by something as simple as following the system or process that the recipe clearly spells out. That should be easy enough, right?

Push yourself to reach your goals by using a counting system. I'm a passionate reader and joined a book club in an effort to read more interesting and enriching books. It worked. I read and enjoy books that never would have been a personal choice. A typical month included the book club selection as well as another book of my own choosing. A second book club increased that number to three per month. Thirty-six books a year was in striking distance of one book a week, a fact that may have gone unnoticed had I not been counting. I have made fifty-two books annually my reading goal for several years now and have accomplished it only once so far. Falling a little short of the goal still puts me much further ahead than I would be without focusing on the numbers. The addition of so many more great books has dramatically improved my scope of interest and my knowledge in general.

Jerry Bruckner, author of *The Success Formula for Personal Growth* (2010), wrote, "For a successful life or a successful business measure what you want to improve." We do what we measure. I set a goal to walk ten miles per week and purchased a pedometer to measure my favorite walking trails and neighborhood loops. I identified one-, two-, and three-mile routes and started adding up the miles weekly. It always seemed that I covered more ground than the numbers indicated. The weeks passed quickly and Saturday often found me taking makeup walks to reach my goal of ten miles.

If you apply this same simple system to business, you will be amazed at the results. My business success in the first few years can be attributed almost entirely to beginner's luck. I would bump into a neighbor at the grocery store who would express the need to sell their home. Or a conversation at our community pool would generate leads and sales. My business was not being built on purpose until I started counting. How many doors did I have to knock on to set an appointment? How many presentations must I make to get a contract? How many listings would it take to reach my annual goal? And eventually, how many escrows must close, at what price, to reach my income goal?

The possibilities for improving your life using the counting method are endless. Counting keeps your level of awareness tuned in to what is important. If you are focused on the goal, it becomes almost a game to push yourself a little further to hit the target. Keeping track keeps you accountable.

Set benchmarks to track your success. It is important to analyze your progress and evaluate your systems to measure improvement. When you recognize an area of your life that you wish to improve, prepare an action plan with step-by-step procedures and time lines. As you reach each target or time line, analyze your progress and adjust as necessary. When you measure your success, you can make a decision to continue at the same rate, step the pace up or down, or replace the process with something that will be a better fit for you.

No matter what systems you use, remember to minimize and streamline the process, wherever possible. This might take time to perfect, but don't give up. If you feel resistance and the system isn't making your life easier, go back to square one and work on a smaller challenge. When each recurring event in your daily life is systemized, you will accomplish more, in less time, with much less frustration along the way. You will fully enjoy the fruits of your labor and that positive, confident feeling that results from taking charge of the direction of your life.

Eight

Create White Space

"It is my observation that too many of us
are spending money we haven't earned to
buy things we don't need to impress people
we don't like."

— WILL ROGERS, HUMORIST AND SOCIAL
COMMENTATOR

The best way I know to enjoy an organized life is to maintain control of your environment. When you simplify your life, you feel balanced, contented, and in control. In reference to page layout, white space is the unmarked area of the page; margins, and the space between lines, graphics, and columns. It is just as important to the printed piece as the written words. I use the term metaphorically to conceptualize an uncluttered environment—clean, organized space in your home, office, calendar, and mind.

I maintain a fairly well-organized home and office by creating an environment with a place for everything, and everything in its place. It's a continuous work in progress. Nobody's perfect. Have you ever mislaid your car keys and spent valuable time searching for them? And what's worse, have you done the same thing the next day? Searching for critical items, like keys, will not only make you late, but will completely frazzle you and set the mood for the day—most likely not a positive mood. Have you ever been on an important phone conversation and wanted to jot down a few notes only to realize once again that the pen in your drawer is out of ink? We all do this. We try the pen, realize it's empty, and toss it back in the drawer. So a useless pen is returned to its proper place, but the car keys could be anywhere. If either of these scenarios sounds familiar, you need to get organized. Simply put, clutter clouds our thinking. A messy home or office does not demonstrate how busy you are.

Self-organization starts here. I know it's not easy, but it is absolutely essential to eliminate the clutter in our lives, both physical and mental. When we accomplish this, we can enjoy harmony in our lives, also physically and mentally. The famous architect Mies van der Rohe stated, "Less is more". I embrace that concept. Try re-gifting, recycling, or simply tossing out one item for every new item you purchase. It can be that easy.

I am an advocate of the power of feng shui and have experienced firsthand the positive results that it can bring. It is based on the premise that the way you arrange furniture and objects in your home or office affects the chi, or energy flow, of the room. When you make changes in your environment, you change the chi. Energy, whether it's good or bad, will directly affect you personally, which in turn will impact your thoughts and actions. The more positive your thoughts and actions are, the more successful you will be professionally, and the more content you will be in life.

Feng shui has nothing to do with religion and it is not a passing fad. It is an art and a science that has been practiced in China for more than three thousand years. The first step is to get rid of everything that you own, but don't love. Look at everything as if for the first time. It's eye-opening to see what we can accumulate over time. Begin the process by clearing out excess possessions. Open up the windows and blinds and let in as much natural light and fresh air as possible. I don't pretend to be an expert, but I do know that making a few simple changes and creating an open, airy setting will immediately improve the chi in your surroundings. Good energy created by a balanced environment will bring you harmony and peace.

White space is a wonderful thing. I have read books on organization where the author recommends taking everything out of the closet and replacing only what you truly need and regularly wear. I tried this method and failed. I got the clothes out of the closet, but ran out of time (or possibly energy and focus) before the mission was complete. Days later I was still dressing from the piles on the floor.

My system for cleaning out the closet is not so overwhelming. Start with one small area. The first goal might be to make some sense of your shoes. Remove all of your shoes from the closet so that you can evaluate them in groups according to need and style. If you have accumulated too many of one kind, sort them and thin them out. Plan to keep the shoes that you enjoy wearing and that are comfortable. Those criteria are critical. Keep them only if they feel good and make you feel good.

I am a very frugal person and feel the need to get my money's worth out of anything I purchase. I am guilty of keeping clothes that don't look good on me, or that I don't feel good in, because I feel the need to wear them a few more times in an effort to justify the cost of purchase. That is not only false economy, but it's also pointless. Why would I wear something that is wrong for me when I have other options? Gift those items to someone who will look great in them and let him or her eke out a little more value. If you don't have anyone to give them to, schedule a donation to Goodwill or one of the many organizations that would benefit from your discards. Having a pickup scheduled will provide a deadline to keep the job on track. It is liberating to know that those outfits are going where they will be appreciated.

Pare down your possessions to just what you need and no more. Maybe you have a closet full of clothes that are in the right place, but you don't need them all. Make the decision to clean out your closet one rung, drawer, or shelf at a time. I had plans to visit my mother the other day and I knew that my similar-sized sister would be there, too. I donate my hand-me-downs to her and she picks and chooses a few things and then passes the rest to various friends to do the same. I had only a few minutes, so I grabbed two shopping bags and whipped through my closet taking the items that I pass on every morning to get to the clothes that I actually wear. I didn't have time to think or second guess my decisions. I just filled the bags and left the house. It felt great! Five minutes of purging and I created white space in my closet. The following morning I rearranged the clothes a little, removed the extra hangers, and moved on.

Work through your closet systematically, one small area at a time. It's a process and it gets easier as you go. When organizing this way, I go through my belongings once and make a stack to give away or donate, put back the ones worth keeping, and move to the next area. Once I get into the "less is more" groove, I can revisit areas already culled and find many more items that I can easily live without. This is an effortless way to maintain an organized closet at all times.

This system works in other areas where we are apt to accumulate excess, including the office, kitchen, and garage. Let go of possessions that do not enhance your life. Pick one small area to attack and make a quick decision about each item. Either toss it into the trash container, add it to the donation box, or put it back in its place. My kitchen has one of everything required, not several. The drawers are filled like a puzzle. Some items are side by side, some perpendicular. All items are easy to spot when I need them. When something is used, it is returned to the same location in the drawer or cupboard. Everything stays neat and at my fingertips. Try it! When you open a drawer and see white space you will feel like you can breathe. Don't overthink it. Just do it.

Creating white space requires that we reduce physical clutter by getting rid of things that take up space. Also consider eliminating things that require maintenance, take up precious time, or in some way complicate our lives. I am a dedicated online shopper. It has made my life easier in countless ways. When John and I planned our wedding, we set a date that didn't leave much time for preparation and implementation. We were both very busy in those days, but determined to make the day special in every way. I bought my wedding dress online at Nordstrom.com one evening after work. The next evening I ordered my perfect off-white strappy satin heels from Zappos. This was followed by an order for two hundred peonies from an online floral wholesaler in Vermont, which were delivered as tight buds a few days early to ensure that they would be in perfect bloom for the occasion. We selected and ordered the wine online and arranged for delivery the day before for chilling purposes. From the privacy of our home, we were able to complete all that and more. Christmas and birthday shopping are accomplished in just the same way.

Online shopping has definitely created white space in the form of time, but as with so many things in life, there is a trade-off. Whenever I order something online, I am placed on at least one, sometimes several, e-mail lists. My inbox is inundated with correspondence from each site visited. When checking my e-mail, the first few minutes are spent deleting dozens of unwanted solicitations from online vendors trying to generate business. I unsubscribe to e-mails on a regular basis. When I check my inbox, it's manageable and the e-mails received are appropriate and interesting. I have successfully created much-needed white space in this area of my life.

In the late 1990s and early 2000s, there was an online grocery service in our area. With a family of five hearty eaters, I was instantly hooked. I would sit in front of the computer in my bathrobe and slippers perusing my cookbooks. Once I decided what recipes I would make that week, I ordered the ingredients along with our regular staples. All of those groceries including heavy cases of water would be delivered right to my kitchen counter. They didn't charge anything for the service and wouldn't even accept a tip. If it seems too good to be true.... I wasn't surprised when the company went out of business, proving yet again that it's not feasible to sustain a business long term without creating a consistent revenue stream. It was, however, great while it lasted.

Create white space in the relationship sector of your life. Eliminate relationships and affiliations that don't enrich your life. Some people take up time and drain our energy without giving anything in return. They may be wonderful people or organizations, but when it's clear that you have outgrown them, it's time to move on. Distance yourself gracefully either by letting them go or by relegating them to a reduced capacity in your life where they use up less space. Have you heard the saying, "It's okay to walk out of someone's life if you don't feel you belong in it anymore"?

Create white space in your calendar. The temptation to-day is to overbook our schedules because, after all, time is money. However, we need to leave room for those unanticipated events that pop up in the course of a day. When you are stretched too thin, you feel stressed, worn out, and out of balance. Back-to-back appointments don't allow time to check e-mails, return phone calls, or put out the occasional fire. They also don't allow for preparation time so that you can offer the consistent service your clients have grown to expect. Take some time to identify activities that have lost their luster or are no longer aligned with your goals. Cancel them as soon as you responsibly can do so. Fill that time doing things that are meaningful to you, move you closer to your goals, or simply allow an opportunity to relax.

Take control of your time and run your business without it running you…ragged.

Nine

Consistency Counts

"My name is CONSISTENCY. I am related to
SUCCESS.
We should hang out more than...every once
in a while."

— KIM GARST, SOCIAL MEDIA BUSINESS
CONSULTANT (2014)

Consistency takes willpower in the beginning, but in time, "habits of life" form and you are on your way to a less stressful, more successful existence. Doing the same things over and over until you do them without thinking streamlines your existence and sets proper expectations. Consistency requires a system. This SYSTEM will Save You Stress Time Energy Money. I know acronyms are a little cheesy, but this one might help you to focus and stay on track.

Remember the last time you visited a spa? You may have experienced something like this:

A gracious receptionist greeted you at the desk and checked you in. Everyone spoke in hushed tones and music played softly in the background. You were ushered back to your locker, handed a warm, clean robe and slippers, and left alone to change into something more comfortable. She took the time to show you the shower and restroom area, the beauty station to repair hair and makeup after your treatment, and offered the use of the jetted tub and sauna rooms to prolong your spa experience. Once you were comfy, you were led to a "quiet" room, offered a sparkling glass of cucumber-lemon water, and left to fully relax before your treatment.

You enjoyed such tranquility on your first visit that a return visit was scheduled for another dose of pampering. However, this time it was busy and the receptionist was trying to do too many things at once. You were rushed through the arrival process and instead of being escorted to the changing area, she waved her hand in the general direction and told you to enter the door on the left to the locker room. You searched for and located your locker, found a robe and oversized slippers, and changed. You went to the waiting room, poured a glass of water, and waited patiently to be called.

If the visits were reversed, you may not have been disappointed the first time, but you also wouldn't be a raving fan. The experience may not even have ranked high enough to warrant a second visit. You most certainly would not go out of your way to recommend it to your friends.

I consider myself a service provider, not a salesperson. The easiest way to build a long-term, successful business is to foster referrals from past satisfied clients. Commit to building rapport right from the start. It's as easy as spending a few minutes getting to know the customer and their needs prior to jumping into the car to show them homes.

- **Have they been prequalified?**
  It's a mistake to show homes that are higher than their price range. It's too disappointing when reality hits and they can't afford the house with the pool, fourth bedroom, or view.

- **What are their priorities?**
  Do both parties agree on those priorities? They may have qualified for a home in the price range for the size home they want, but beyond that, will they be willing to compromise on lot size, view, and additional amenities?

- **Are schools important?**
  If schoolchildren are involved, this is a critical question and will be much appreciated by the parents.

- **Is drive time to work a consideration?**
  The buyers may not think about this until they have committed to the purchase and feel the first pang of buyer's remorse.

There are a number of critical questions to be answered before you go in search of the house of their dreams. Imagine if your Realtor spent a few minutes asking those questions and then thoughtfully scheduled homes that were appropriate for you and your family. It would probably be a very good experience. In fact, it would be so good that you would tell your friends about it. And when they are ready to make a move, they might decide that this type of personalized service would be beneficial for them and make an appointment with your Realtor, too.

Now imagine that yesterday was a busy day for the Realtor. She had an escrow cancel at the last minute and her next best prospects listed their home with someone else. She was not on her game and didn't properly prepare for the meeting with your friends. Because you shared an experience that exceeded your expectations, your friends were looking forward to the same level of attention. However, they were disappointed.

Preparation is directly related to providing consistency. Yesterday ended. The only thing needed prior to the appointment was thorough preparation in an effort to provide a consistent experience for the new customers. That is how reputations are made. At the end of the day, a good reputation is essential to building and sustaining a successful business. My example is real estate related because I maintained a long-term, successful career in real estate by protecting my reputation at all times. The message is relevant and should not be underestimated regardless of the industry you serve.

Whatever it is you want to achieve, you can do it, starting today. Practice makes perfect. I am a big fan of the 100 Day Challenge. If you google it, you will be inspired by the amazing success stories that you find. The 100 Day Challenge asks you to do just one thing, and that is to be the best that you can be today, in one small area of your life, and to repeat that process every day for the duration of the challenge.

A challenge like this requires steadfast commitment, focused vision, and unwavering determination. It must be based on something you are passionate about. Without passion, you will never live up to your fullest potential. To quote my favorite children's song, the "Hokey Pokey," you must "put your whole self in." If your career/personal/spiritual/intellectual world is not igniting your passion, it's time to fire things up. Revise, reframe, and redefine it until you are unstoppable.

Give some serious thought to just one part of your life that you want to improve. You must truly want it or you will not successfully complete the challenge. It's easiest if you start with the end in mind. Where do you want to be at the end of the challenge? Now consider what you must do daily to reach your goal in one hundred days. Doing this makes each step manageable. Our days are full, so the only way this will work in the long term is to make your starting point as easy as possible.

Do you want to improve your health?

- Instead of pledging to lose five pounds in a hundred days, commit to making a change that will cause that to happen. Try replacing something less healthy with one serving of fruit or vegetables per day, or eliminating one processed food daily.
- Go for a walk or visit the gym.
- Give up soda, coffee, or fast food for a hundred days. Once it's a habit, you'll wonder why you didn't do it sooner.
- If you have trouble getting to the gym, challenge yourself to at least three sit-ups per day. It sounds like it's such an inconsequential challenge that it won't make a difference, but by the end of the challenge you will be doing many times that without breaking a sweat. It's important to keep your commitment so simple that it's easier to keep it than to let yourself down.

Do you want to save money?

- Start today by committing to brewing your own coffee instead of stopping at Starbucks.
- Limit dining out to once a week, or pack your lunch during the week. If you do eat out, try sharing a meal or ordering from the happy hour or appetizer menu.
- Commit to a hundred days without shopping for yourself. If you clean out your closet, you will probably discover a number of wardrobe choices you have forgotten you even own (see chapter 7).

- Save your change in a jar and at the end of the challenge, add this and any other money you saved on purpose to your retirement account (see chapter 14), vacation, or Christmas fund.

Do you want to reach out to your client base?

- Stock up on note cards and don't let a day go by that at least one person isn't blessed with a personal note from you (see chapter 3).
- Commit to calling a minimum of three past clients per day (see chapter 7).
- Challenge yourself to drop by the home or office of at least one client each day to say hello and wish them well. This will make a difference in more ways than one.

Do you want to learn a second language or get better at your own?

- Commit to listening to training tapes a minimum of fifteen minutes per day while you exercise or during drive time.
- Building language skills can be as simple as adding one word a day to your vocabulary. There's an app for that.

Do you want to write a book or a blog?

- Pledge to write a minimum of fifty words per day. The idea is that if you sit down to write fifty words, you will usually write more. If you are truly struggling and can come up with only one paragraph, you are still that much closer to your goal. As the challenge progresses, the process will become easier.

- Google *WordPress* or a similar blogging platform and set up a blog. Do something every day to make your blog compelling. Set it up, add content, get the word out, and so on.

Do you want to become a reader?

- Start by reading a minimum of ten pages per day. This might require getting up a few minutes earlier in the morning, eliminating a little TV at the end of the day, or both. The results can be measured by the books you finish during the challenge plus the added benefit of better habits at the beginning and end of the day. This could be life changing.
- Listening to books on tape counts. Listen and learn while you take your walk or run, before bed, or whenever you can carve out a few minutes.

Do you need more clients in your pipeline?

- Find a way to meet one new person per day. Go where the people are and join the conversation.
- Once you build your client base, you can arrange to meet with one person face to face per day. Bond over a cup of coffee. Imagine the satisfied customers and referrals you will create from this type of personalized service!

Whatever you decide to do, you must pledge to do it every day for a hundred days. Something wonderful happens along the way. You build momentum and form habits. By the end of the challenge, you will have embedded in your psyche a powerful life habit that is as much a part of your day as brushing your teeth or making your bed.

My first commitment to the challenge was a pledge to exercise on my recumbent bike daily for one hundred days. The commitment was not for a particular length of time or for a certain distance. It was simply a commitment to get on it and move. To make it more attractive I decided to read while exercising. Yes, the benefits of multitasking have been debunked, and focusing on just one thing at a time has been shown to be more valuable, but combining reading and exercising is a real win-win for me. I often extend my workout to complete a chapter or finish a book. The challenge wasn't met every single day, but I managed to exercise for at least a short amount of time most of the hundred days. Two excellent habits were reinforced to the point that I actually look forward to reading and working out regularly.

Now that you get the idea, it is time to take action! Are you willing to make a commitment to yourself and to the next one hundred days of your life? If so, ask yourself the following thought provoking questions:

- ➢ What is your intention?
- ➢ In what area of your life do you have a burning desire to effect one small, positive change?

> ➢ What is the one thing that you will commit to doing every day during the challenge?

Start today. Do it again tomorrow…and every day for the next one hundred days. Challenging yourself on a regular basis will help to avoid burnout. Fatigue in the form of burnout feels like "been there, done that." When the highs are gone, dissatisfaction sets in and we no longer strive for success. Once the newness wears off, we stop doing the tasks that worked for us in the beginning, and we become distracted and concentrate on the wrong things. Eventually those diversions fail to fuel our fire and we look for something newer still. Where exactly did that wonderful rush go and why can't we get it back? Is that all there is? Every day? From now on? You feel the let-down and you become tired of trying. The solution is to understand that you constantly need to test your abilities and to figure out how you can integrate challenge into all areas of your life.

The best way to feed our need for creativity and challenge is to step back and do a little planning and goal setting. Make and keep a daily schedule. That's easier to say than to do, but it is critical to long-term success. Consistency in your daily routine will guarantee success. This is the perfect time to find a mentor or an accountability partner. Challenge each other to stay on track and remain focused on your goals.

Remember to start small, keep it simple, and fully commit. Once you have conquered that first habit, raise the bar and set the next challenge. There is always room for improvement, so why not make a game of it? When you do this, you are living the life Mahatma Gandhi had in mind when he counseled, "You must be the change you wish to see in the world". If that thought is too lofty, think "lather, rinse, repeat." That will get you to a better version of you.

A lways
S eek
K nowledge

Ten

Stay in Curious Mode

"Anyone who stops learning is old, whether
at twenty or eighty.
Anyone who keeps learning stays young."

— HENRY FORD, AMERICAN INDUSTRIALIST

Be a lifelong learner by remaining in curious mode at all times. There is something very empowering about learning. It broadens horizons, provides more opportunities for advancement, and generally enhances our understanding of the world. Life is so much more interesting when we remain open every day to new ideas and personal development. The world is moving so fast that if you become complacent for even a short while, life might pass you by.

My parents were advocates of formal education and encouraged their children to go to college to create a solid base from which to build successful careers and lives. Good grades were expected. Formal education does open doors, provides more and better choices, and lays the groundwork for us to live up to our potential, but learning doesn't stop there. There are many ways outside of school to improve and expand knowledge and skills.

When raising my family, I called it "falling forward." If my children wanted to take music lessons, join a sports team, or follow their passion du jour, I did my best to make it happen. There were, however, rules attached. Whatever they started required a commitment to the length of the course or season. Quitting prior to completion was not allowed. Not bendy enough for gymnastics? Complete the sessions you signed up for and move on to something else. Soccer not your thing? Finish the season and "fall forward" to another activity. Being curious and trying new activities allowed them to fine-tune their talents and strengths. Some pastimes turn into lifelong passions, such as playing guitar and surfing did for my boys. It is amazing how often experimenting with something that doesn't resonate at the time will randomly, at some future point, be put to good use. Even a minimal amount of knowledge, acquired while dabbling, will serve you well.

My grandfather taught me the importance of being open to new experiences. He was a true scholar. He retired from real estate sales and development in his fifties and he spent the next thirty years traveling the world with my grandmother. They weren't typical travelers. When they visited Africa they steered clear of the American-style hotels and stayed in tree houses or mud huts with the natives. My grandfather was more of an adventurer than my poor grandmother, but she was a remarkably good sport. When preparing for a trip, he studied the culture, beliefs, and history of the people he would be visiting. Having an awareness and understanding prior to the visit positioned him to absorb so much more about his exotic hosts and their surroundings. This knowledge provided tremendous insight into their foreign adventures.

Research like my grandfather's is so easy in today's lightning-fast information age. Google puts the world literally at our fingertips. If a question is posed with no clear answer, google it. That's one method of learning.

Look around you. So many people go through life with their cell phone blocking their view. My husband and I recently sat at a sidewalk café in beautiful Napa Valley and watched the world go by. It was one of those glorious spring days that make you want to play outside. People were out, but not one person who passed by seemed to be aware of their delightful surroundings. Every person who walked past us was either texting or talking on the phone. I am not exaggerating. There is so much to be learned if we pay attention and live in the moment.

Recently, I was scheduled for a medical test and sat patiently in the hospital waiting room. In the center of the room, there was a display that looked like a computerized version of a huge fish tank. The sign described it as "interactive media." There were no fish, but there were computerized "bubbles" effervescing in the "tank." Inside some of the bubbles were icons depicting different areas of health. If you tapped on the glass, some of the bubbles would burst and a video or message would pop up. The kids were fascinated by it and so was I. They were having fun popping the bubbles and I was having fun observing what popped out. Did you know that our nose and ears continue to grow throughout our life, but our eyes stay the same size? I knew about the ears and nose, and find that a little bit unsettling, but I had no idea about the eyes. That must be why toddlers' eyes are always so amazing. They haven't grown into them yet. Who knows if there will ever be a use for this bit of information or if I will even remember to share it if the appropriate opportunity arises? Well, as it turns out, there is, because at least a few of you may not have been aware of that fact. The bottom line is, by being open and aware, I learned at least one new thing, which has now been shared with you.

My husband opened my eyes to the beauty of the desert. I was never very impressed with the desert landscape which seemed stark and a little austere to me. I didn't give desert plants credit for not just surviving, but also actually thriving with very little water in extreme heat. John loves the desert and is very knowledgeable about the local flora and fauna. We would take long walks and he would point out remarkable plants. I would see a thorny cactus and he would notice the delicate, but vibrant flowers, blooming amid the thorns. He loves the Zen-like ridges left by the gardener's rakes and the fact that everything is so "buttoned down," his words for neat and trim. All of a sudden, there was beauty everywhere I looked. The flowers bloom brilliantly all year long, and where the rugged mountains meet the sky, the blue is intensely blue.

Yes, it's unbearably hot for three months of the year, but it is also peaceful when the season ends and the snowbirds return to their homes in the cold weather states. I am so grateful that John took the time to introduce me to that beautiful new world. I might have lived my entire life unaware that such desert splendor existed.

Practice the fine art of listening as an efficient learning tool. I maintained excellent grades in high school, but it required hours of homework and independent study on my part. My valuable class time was spent passing notes back and forth to my friends instead of listening to what the teacher was trying to communicate. At college I met students who were more mature and serious about learning and soon discovered that if one actually paid attention during class, it wasn't necessary to start from scratch to prepare for exams. The professors taught us what we needed to know. We just had to listen. It was a new concept to me, one that served me well from that point on.

It's easy to fall into the habit of forming a response while the person you are conversing with is still talking. When we do that, we assume we know what they are going to say. Hearing and listening are not the same. Have you ever asked someone how they are and then, before listening to their answer, you gave a rote response assuming that they were going to say "Fine, thanks"? What if they weren't fine and you didn't wait to hear it? Give others the opportunity to share their thoughts without rushing them. Develop the habit of waiting for one beat before you answer. Listen carefully and pay attention to what is being said and, if necessary, ask clarifying questions. Listening to people's needs and responding appropriately will earn and keep friends and customers.

I conducted a workshop where we discussed continuing education as an ongoing necessity in an ever-changing environment. The conversation segued into things that we, as individuals, wanted to learn. One person shared that he had purchased a guitar some time ago and hadn't taken the time to learn to play. I suggested he schedule some time with my son who is an excellent mentor. When it was my turn, I mentioned that I wanted to learn to make cheese. As luck would have it, one of the attendees had a cheese-making "kit" and offered to help me make ricotta and mozzarella. We had fun during the cheese-making process and I was able to produce a marvelous spinach and sausage lasagna featuring two types of homemade cheese. The point is to push yourself to learn new things. And then push yourself some more.

Learning for the sake of learning builds confidence and self-esteem. It benefits networking immensely. Even a rudimentary understanding of a subject will allow you to strike up a conversation with someone who is an expert in that field. Knowing the right questions to ask will let them know you are interested in hearing what they have to say. It gives you common ground to connect with people and is a wonderful way to initiate a professional relationship or friendship.

Trying to keep up with the rapid changes in the business world can be quite daunting. In an effort to stay relevant, I decided to start a blog, but had no idea how to go about it. I made a list of the steps necessary to get started. The first phase was to secure a domain name through GoDaddy. Next, I researched the available blogging platforms and selected WordPress as the site and BlueHost to host it. Those decisions would appear to have been made based on a clear understanding of the options, but the truth is, I have no idea how I ended up there. I couldn't go back now and reconstruct the path taken. Somehow, a few random clicks and credit card authorizations added up to an almost-functioning blog. It was a daunting process. I googled for support at every turn. When stuck, I called the helpline, feverishly noting the instructions they gave me. As soon as I hung up the phone, I googled the words they used, then called back using more effective words to explain the problem. It was a huge learning curve, and with all that help, I was able to make it happen—posting, adding photos, setting up site analytics, managing comments, and thoroughly enjoying the feeling of accomplishment that came with the results.

Staying ahead of the curve is not easy. It is, however, vital to maintaining relevance. Keep an open mind and delight in new and interesting ideas. Be patient when you suffer growing pains and stay strong when you feel vulnerable. Understanding new concepts and philosophies will not only make you more interesting, but you will be more valuable to your clients, employer, and friends. Mahatma Gandhi said, "Live as if you were to die tomorrow. Learn as if you were to live forever". The constant pursuit of new adventures in learning requires courage and confidence. These are values that are essential to self-organization and a better version of you.

Pros   Cons

It's time to decide

Eleven

Decide to Be Decisive

"On an important decision one rarely has
100% of the information needed for a good
decision no matter how much one spends or
how long one waits. And, if one waits too
long, he has a different problem and has to
start over.
This is the terrible dilemma of the hesitant
decision maker."

— ROBERT K. GREENLEAF, *SERVANT AS LEADER*
(2002)

Make good decisions. Actually, just make a decision and move on it, even if you aren't completely convinced it is absolutely the perfect decision. It is easier to adjust your focus once you have created momentum by moving forward. When you are up and running, your best course of action will become more apparent. If you are stuck in indecision mode, you can get "poisoned by possibilities." Too many choices make it difficult to see the best way. Either they all look good or they all look bad and the available options rarely include the perfect answer when you need it. Allan Rufus, author of *The Master's Sacred Knowledge* (2012), discusses personal development through self-discovery. He contends that "life is like a game of chess. To win you have to make a move. Knowing which way to move comes with insight and knowledge, and by learning the lessons that are accumulated along the way. We become each and every piece within the game called life."

People who have trouble making decisions aren't necessarily taking the easy road. They truly agonize about making the best decision they possibly can. But until you put it out there and test it, there is no way of knowing if you have made a good decision or not. So you are caught in a holding pattern. You haven't made the decision to try, and until you do, you won't know if it is the right move or the wrong one. That's a real dilemma.

Either way, failing to decide is not an option. Sitting on the fence with analysis paralysis every time a decision needs to be made is both exhausting and nonproductive. If there is a choice that suffices or is good enough, go with it, and although you really want to revisit your decision to see if you would have made the same one given a second chance, don't do it. Overthinking guarantees a stalemate; you can't move forward and you can't move back once self-doubt sets in. Make the good-enough decision, and run, don't walk. No more hesitation.

There are so many people who would love to take a chance and change careers, or grab at least one brass ring on their journey through life, but for numerous reasons they just can't make the move. It's not the right time, there's no guarantee of success, and so on. We know there are no guarantees in life and every move is fraught with peril, but risks are what life is all about and some are worth taking. Trust that a net will appear when you need it. The alternative is never having even tried.

My father is a brilliant man, but not a decisive one. I was young and impressionable during the Cold War years. The adults were all abuzz about what to do as the threat of war loomed. We went to bed at night worrying that nuclear war was imminent. My poor dad. He must have been completely overwhelmed to begin with, raising six children on a civil servant's income. If that wasn't bad enough, he now faced the responsibility of making the best decision possible to keep his family safe in the event of nuclear war. I'm certain that was more than he signed up for and he deserves to be applauded for even trying to do the right thing.

Every night after work, he pored over maps and manuals and listened to news programs trying to determine what options were available in his quest to keep us safe. According to his research, Eureka, California, and New Zealand would be the two safest places on earth to avoid the danger of fallout. He gave serious thought to moving us to one of those two places. The other consideration was to build a bomb shelter in our backyard. Can you imagine six kids and two adults spending any amount of time together in a backyard bomb shelter?

I'm claustrophobic, so if that was his final decision, I would be forced to run away (hopefully, to Eureka or New Zealand). He worried about what he should do for months, but never made a decision. Thankfully, John F. Kennedy stared down the Russians during the Cuban Missile Crisis and, disaster averted, the necessity of making any kind of decision passed.

This is an extreme example and in all fairness, I'm sure even the most decisive people were stumped by this one. As a kid, the only thing worse than my fear of the atom bomb was my fear of having to move and change schools. As a parent, I am very grateful to my dad for putting himself through such an excruciating exercise on behalf of his family. My point is, if you wait long enough, decisions will be made for you and not all of them will work out in your best interest. I was very grateful for this particular missed opportunity, but how many others were there that would have been life changing in a good way?

It is on us to step up and be the leaders we were meant to be. People are thirsting for leadership. Our family, clients, and friends could use a little infusion of confidence in the face of decisions that must be made. You can help people make good decisions through what I refer to as "guided discovery." It will be easier for them to make prudent choices if you offer them enough information to make educated decisions for themselves.

When representing buyers and sellers, my first response to a problem was to take ownership of it. Even though it was not truly my problem, it was my responsibility to help solve it. I usually had a preferred solution in mind, but the ultimate decision was theirs. If I made a decision on their behalf and it was wrong, I would be to blame. If they made a decision based on facts and information that were available at the time and it turned out to be wrong, well, we tried. I guided them to what seemed to be the best decision by educating them with current facts and by sharing my past experiences. Sometimes my guidance didn't help them discover what seemed to me to be the best decision, but I was satisfied that they had been properly represented.

Guided discovery works well with children and very well with spouses. Just drop a few hints. It may take a nudge or two, but all of a sudden, a lightbulb will come on and voilà! They'll come up with a great idea all on their own. Now, why didn't I think of that?

Some people would rather complain than decide. The Realtors I managed knew better than to come to me with a predicament without also bringing several viable solutions to discuss. They were usually able to identify the best possible resolution to the problem once they talked through the projected outcome of each choice. In this way I was more of a sounding board or guide to the right decision than the decision maker. File this under the heading of "teach a man to fish…"

If you find yourself obsessing over even the smallest decisions, ask yourself a few questions.

- **How important is this decision?**
  If you're having trouble deciding what to order for lunch, it's OK to make a bad decision. You can order something else tomorrow. The decision will not have any impact on your life. If it is a life-changing decision,

call for a lifeline from someone you trust. Don't ask for the opinion of just anyone and everyone. If they don't have a vested interest in your success/failure, their opinion may just further complicate the issue.

- **What's the worst possible outcome that could result if the wrong decision is made?**
  How high are the risks, really? If the consequences are not life altering, you might be able to live with making a bad decision long enough to adjust your direction.

- **What are the alternatives?**
  The alternatives might not offer the perfect solution either, but they may offer an opportunity to buy time until you can get clear on your direction.

- **Do you trust your gut?**
  Sometimes everything points in one direction, but it just doesn't feel quite right. In most cases it is a good idea to trust your instincts and wait, if possible, until your direction is clear.

We can thank Benjamin Franklin for his very practical process for decision making. It involves one sheet of paper and two columns. In one column, list all of the pros associated with the decision you are wrestling with, and in the other column, list the cons. This usually makes the choice very clear. If that doesn't work, ask someone you trust to listen while you verbally weigh the pros and cons to identify the best choice. The silent partner doesn't necessarily even have to contribute; he or she simply needs to be a good listener. The best decision at the time, with the information you have, will generally become apparent. Once that happens, act on it before you talk yourself out of it.

You may remember the late 1970s and early 1980s when the American automobile industry was struggling to stay solvent in a weak economy. Chrysler Corporation was on the brink of bankruptcy. It was suffering from poor leadership, no viable plans to keep up with the competition, and design flaws in its current models. In other words, not much on the horizon to generate interest or customer loyalty. Then, just when it seemed all was lost, Lee Iacocca rose to the occasion and rescued the company. He had made a name for himself with the introduction of the Mustang at Ford and was viewed as the perfect fit to turn the company around. He did just that, in record time, and was praised as quite a hero. Well, he was a hero for a while, anyway. He is also remembered for making a few bad investment decisions that unraveled much of the good he was praised for.

Whether he was making good decisions or bad ones, Iacocca was known as a decisive, quick-thinking leader with unconventional ideas that usually worked. When it comes to making good decisions, he famously declared, "If I had to sum up the qualities that make a good manager, I'd say that it comes down to decisiveness. You can use the fanciest computers to gather the numbers, but in the end you have to set a timetable and act" (1984). Decide today to take charge of your life. Decide to do better and to be better, and don't look back.

Personal
Responsibility
In
Delivering
Excellence

Twelve

Commit to Excellence

"The quality of a person's life is in direct
proportion to their commitment to
excellence, regardless of their chosen field
of endeavor."

— Vince Lombardi, American Football Player
and Renowned Coach

Excellence means we demand more of ourselves than
others demand of us. It means doing the right things
when no one is looking and doing the little things until they
add up to big things. It does not mean we are perfect.
Striving for excellence and maintaining high standards is
a very good thing. Striving for perfection is a recipe for
disaster. Accept your imperfections and acknowledge your
weaknesses. Either work on strengthening them or simply
play to your strengths. Trust me when I say there will always
be someone younger, thinner, smarter, or more successful

than you. It's OK to be happy for them and content with yourself at the same time.

We all have received many holiday cards with those dreadful annual letters where some relative or acquaintance unselfconsciously brags about his or her family's accomplishments over the past year. The children excelled in school and on the sports field, their glamorous vacations were Shangri-la-ish, and the breadwinner received a huge promotion. Of course, stunning photos were included to further salt the wound.

I put Facebook in the same category, but unlike holiday letters, it can erode your confidence year round. Check Facebook at any time, on any day, and the oversharing by your friends might discourage you. Your otherwise satisfactory life suddenly feels small and insignificant. Your daughter's wedding was a beautiful, intimate family affair. All the others seem to be larger-than-life extravaganzas. You went camping and they went to Paris. Love the life that you have created. Your camping trip may have been just the stress-free, low-cost getaway that you needed to rejuvenate you and yours. Your Facebook friends may very well arrive home exhausted and in debt. Who knows or cares?

Don't compare your own amazing self to anyone else. When we do that, we always fall short. On the other hand, when we measure ourselves against our own past performance, we are motivated to improve bit by bit until we are excellent. Commit to making small incremental steps toward a better version of you, and over time, you will achieve excellence. Practice self-acceptance, relax your shoulders, and breathe.

By tirelessly self-improving, we build on our accomplishments and raise not just our standards, but the standards of everyone we come into contact with. Aristotle counsels, "We are what we repeatedly do. Excellence, then, is not an act but a habit". Colin Powell thinks along those same lines. He says, "If you are going to achieve excellence in big things, you develop the habit in little matters. Excellence is not an exception, it is a prevailing attitude".

Sarah Ban Breathnach wrote a wonderful book called *Simple Abundance: A Daybook of Comfort and Joy* (1995). I have given this book numerous times as a gift or loaned my well-worn copy to friends who were going through a rough patch in life. It doesn't require tough times to add grace to your life, but this book has proven to be a soothing salve when healing is needed. The book offers sage advice for every day of the year. In 2006 I was definitely in a rough patch. The economy was diving deeper by the day into a prolonged recession and homes weren't selling.

During the real estate heyday of the early 2000s, I invested in real estate, on my own, and at times with a business partner. We resold some homes for profit, exchanged a few in tax-deferred exchanges, and held others as long-term rentals. We purchased with 20 percent down, but values dropped to the point that there wasn't much, if any, equity left. Tenants were struggling to pay their rent or just giving up and not trying to pay at all. Desperate people do desperate things, so many of the finest people dug their heels in and hired attorneys to find loopholes that would allow them to stay in our properties for prolonged periods of time, at our expense.

During those grim financial times, my CPA passed away. I felt the loss personally because he was a dear friend, and professionally because he understood my investments, tax history, and where the bones were buried. I mentioned that some of my investments were sold as 1031 exchanges which would defer taxes due on net gains until a later time. My new CPA questioned whether those exchanges would withstand an IRS audit should I face one. He said the exchanges might stand up under scrutiny, but he couldn't guarantee they wouldn't overturn them given the opportunity. I made the decision to revise my taxes and unwind the tax-deferred sales. My fear was that if there were gray areas, the IRS would certainly rule in their favor and that if they did conduct an audit, it would most likely happen down the road when I was winding down my business. It would be very discouraging to be looking forward to retirement and faced with back taxes, plus interest and penalties. No one likes surprises and I am certainly not comfortable looking over my shoulder.

Revising my taxes resulted in a six-figure tax obligation and the IRS had their hand out immediately. They required huge monthly payments until the full amount was satisfied. Even with a perfect monthly payment record, their policy required that liens be placed on all of my properties. Ouch! If there was equity before, there certainly wasn't now. You get the picture. It was really a rough patch.

In October 2006, I was preparing for an open house, but was not looking forward to it because buyers were few and far between. A shortage of buyers rendered open houses ineffective vehicles for marketing homes. However, a commitment had been made to the sellers and so it would be open as scheduled. As was my custom, I read the page for the day from *Simple Abundance*. More often than not, the message spoke to me and this particular missive was remarkably spot-on. Sarah was talking about the Law of Attraction and the energy that positive thinking creates. Whether consciously or unconsciously, you attract what you focus on—positive or negative. The message that day was to stop thinking in terms of scarcity and to start thinking in terms of abundance. I made the commitment immediately to turn things around and focus only on the good and on what was in my control.

I held the home open, and as expected, it was extremely slow. In this case, the quiet time was welcomed giving me the opportunity to think and get my affairs in order. I sat down with a notebook and set up two columns—assets on one side and responsibilities on the other. I focused on my priorities and made a plan. That piece of paper was front and center at all times for about fifteen months. Selling a few homes resolved the balance of the tax problem. Other homes were sold at a loss to get out from under the monthly commitment of carrying them. Bit by bit I checked things off my worry list. The story in chapter 7 about contacting all of my past clients is a result of this call to arms. The next year found us even deeper in recession. By focusing on abundance and being the best that I could be, I truly did triple my income year over year. There is no doubt, the Law of Attraction works.

It's sad, but true that not everyone shares this quest for excellence. Some people are content settling for the minimum effort required. They are not interested in improving and, unfortunately, it's on us to find a way to work around them. They never manage to get the job done and it falls on their productive coworkers and associates to pick up the slack. The people who don't hold up their end are always the ones who are given a pass because it's just "their way." It's simply expected and accepted that they will not respond to your e-mail or voicemail. They may be a little better about texting, but even then, they aren't stellar. Coincidentally, these are the same people who are constantly preoccupied with their mobile devices as if they are on top of every detail!

I spend literally every day of my life trying to be a better version of the person I was yesterday. Our lives are nothing more than a series of individual days that become weeks, months, and years. They add up to a full life, but each day can be a stand-alone representative of the whole. It's a wonderful habit to rate your life at the end of every day. Did I make a difference? Live healthy? Make someone's day? How could the day have been better? How could I have been better?

It's up to us to accept personal responsibility for our lives. There is always room for improvement and pointing fingers or placing blame stunts our growth. Step up and be accountable. Learn from your mistakes. If circumstances are less than perfect, look for solutions. Playwright George Bernard Shaw admonishes, "People are always blaming their circumstances for what they are. I don't believe in circumstances. The people who get on in this world are the people who get up and look for the circumstances they want, and, if they can't find them, make them".

I refuse to settle for less than my best, every day, and am harder on myself than anyone else would ever be. I seek excellence in everything. That doesn't make me perfect or mean that it's acceptable to stop trying. It calls for PRIDE: Personal Responsibility In Delivering Excellence. There is always room in yesterday's you for improvement, growth, and refinement. According to world champion race driver Mario Andretti, "Desire is the key to motivation, but it's determination and commitment to an unrelenting pursuit of your goal—a commitment to excellence—that will enable you to attain the success you seek".

1. Dream Big
2. Set Goals
3. Take Action

It's about Time

"To have more peace, as well as more time, start by letting go of the notion that time can be manipulated. Then, let go of the idea that it confines you. Instead set out to use the time that is there for its true and best purpose—as the space within which you can live your life to the fullest."

— MICHELLE PASSOFF, *LIGHTEN UP!: FREE YOURSELF FROM CLUTTER* (1998)

We can acknowledge and agree that no matter what happens, time marches on. We can't stop it, but we can control what to do with the time we have. Scheduling our time adds structure to the day and allows us to go from task to task efficiently and effectively. Once your schedule is based on clear thoughtfully set goals, you can enjoy the peace of mind that staying on track provides.

Begin each day by deciding how you will spend your time in pursuit of your goals. Create a comprehensive to-do or "daily accomplishment" list in order of priority and use that to create a schedule that is aligned with your goals and values. Your schedule becomes an essential system that, if followed, guarantees important tasks are completed within the given time frame. That is the simple answer to the not-so-simple question of time management. Consistently strive to complete each task within the time allotted.

I have a visual of my various projects in action. Imagine a farmer driving his John Deere tractor between rows of crops. The tractor has a sprinkler system extending above several rows on each side. It moves very slowly, but with such a wide reach, the farmer can simultaneously nurture all of the plants. In the same way, it is possible to balance a number of areas of your life every day by making small incremental advances toward the achievement of your goals. If you prefer the visual of plates spinning in the air, or irons in the fire, they all illustrate the same idea. Once you have a number of plates in the air, or irons in the fire, focusing a little energy and attention to each one regularly will maintain efficiency and continually move you forward in your chosen direction. In order to accomplish this successfully, you must have a schedule.

At this point, the big picture is clear. You have defined your "why" and your personal goals are firmly in place. There is no longer a need to question who you are, what is important to you, or where you are going. You are in position to successfully harness that previously intangible concept of time by putting what you have learned into practical use. Going forward you will

- ✓ prioritize so that the most important tasks are done first;
- ✓ identify what gets you stuck and get out of the procrastination rut;
- ✓ streamline each task by putting simple systems in place in all areas of your life;
- ✓ create white space by eliminating excess stuff, energy vampires, and unnecessary commitments;
- ✓ exercise willpower to guarantee consistency until lifelong habits are formed;
- ✓ be open minded and committed to learning new things, in new ways, every day;
- ✓ make good-enough decisions, remain confident with those decisions, and not look back; and
- ✓ raise the bar, strive for excellence—not perfection—and be a better version of you.

Wrap all of those components into a daily schedule and you have put into place the time management miracle that may have previously eluded you.

Time is at a premium. There just never seems to be enough of it. Using a schedule to plan your day is practical, easy, and effective, and it enables you to make the most of your time. There are many ways to schedule your to-dos, but the only right way is the one that works for you. Some scheduling systems are overly complex and cumbersome. Keep your plan simple and personal so that you will use it. Although today's smartphones and tablets have excellent apps available, when it comes to scheduling my days and weeks, I still prefer paper. I switched from paper lists and a written schedule to online planning, and back again. There's joy in doodling and adding notes before crossing items off my list. Experiment a little and determine what works best for you. Once you decide, commit to your schedule day in and day out to organize the essentials of your life.

If you pay attention to the minutes, the hours will shape up nicely. Imagine all of the things that you can accomplish in just fifteen minutes. Set a timer and watch what happens. By giving yourself a deadline, you will focus and bring the task in on time. Anything that will take longer than fifteen minutes can be broken down into two or more tasks, each of which should be completed within that time frame. Without a deadline, it could easily take twice as long, or longer. Stop reading right now and take fifteen minutes to advance just one of your goals.

My day is segmented into quarter-hour increments from the first hour until the last. I enjoy my coffee, newspaper, and crossword puzzle for the first forty-five minutes of the day. I'm dressed and ready to hit the ground running within ninety minutes of waking. This includes spending some time attending to household responsibilities such as bed making, room straightening, clothes laundering, plant watering, and dishwasher emptying among other chores. The leisurely start to our morning is a luxury we earned and appreciate now that our kids are grown and gone. It's a wonderful way to ease into the day.

Generating and maintaining a schedule will create more free time and eliminate stress. Spend ten minutes in the evening and write down everything that needs to be done the following day in order of importance. Mentally review each area of your life and identify tasks that will contribute to the accomplishment of each individual goal. If your list is too long, go back through and review and reschedule the nonessentials that can wait for another day. You will no longer waste precious time trying to recall deadlines and commitments. It's important to leave white space in your schedule for unknowns that are sure to pop up. When you take the time to do this, you will wake up poised and ready to execute the tasks needed to complete assignments. You will be able to do this without losing more time wondering what comes first, planning your next move, or worse, backtracking because you forgot to do something. Finish one task and your route is clearly defined by your schedule. Simply focus on the next more important item.

The hardest thing about maintaining a schedule is sticking to it. The only way to stay on track is to handle the diversions as they come up and return to your schedule as soon as possible. Be realistic in your expectations. Not everything will get done every day, but by prioritizing, the important ones will. Scheduling isn't always easy, but it is definitely worth the effort. Think about how much you accomplish the day before you leave for vacation. If you could be that productive every day, you would move mountains. With that in mind, it might be a good idea to include a few more vacations in your schedule.

There are "staging" areas in my home and office to keep things rolling with minimal effort. Whatever is leaving my possession and heading elsewhere is placed in an area near the door. When leaving either home or office, I pick up the items that are there and move them forward. Planning ahead in this way means that I always have the book that needs to be returned to a friend or the library, the clothes for the cleaner, letters to be mailed, and unnecessary or unwanted purchases to be returned. This relieves the frustration of being close enough to cross something off the list, but unprepared to make it happen. Running errands in a circle also saves time. A well-thought-out schedule eliminates backtracking and driving from one end of town to the other. Start at point A, stop at point B, C, and so on, ending back at point A, completing the circle.

It's also about taking time to acknowledge, recognize, and celebrate every success, no matter how small. When we are praised for progress or rewarded for reaching a milestone, we are encouraged and empowered to become even better. Don't wait for others to do this. Feel free to reward yourself for every job well done. Schedule that well-deserved vacation or at least commit to regular play days. Revisit your past and what made you happy and schedule more time for that. The extra time created by following a schedule can be used to start a new hobby, build relationships, or contribute and make a difference. Involving yourself in interests outside of business makes you happier, which attracts even more happiness. Oprah Winfrey believes that "the more you praise and celebrate your life, the more there is in life to celebrate".

Action
Changes
Things

Fourteen

Start Now

"Don't wait until everything is just right. It will never be perfect. There will always be challenges, obstacles and less than perfect conditions. So what. Get started now. With each step you take, you will grow stronger and stronger, more and more skilled, more and more self-confident and more and more successful."

— MARK VICTOR HANSEN, ACTOR AND AUTHOR

I have spent much of my life anticipating my next move, always thinking several moves ahead, as if life were a chess game. When I get married...when we have children...when the children are grown...when I retire and have more time...

I may have missed some of the magic in the everyday moments. Baby books were dutifully maintained for each of my children to record their first smile, first step, first of everything. I was so intent on checking events off the list of things all babies eventually learn that I neglected to fully celebrate each amazing feat as it occurred.

Eckhart Tolle, author of *The Power of NOW: A Guide to Spiritual Enlightenment* (2001), encourages, "Realize deeply that the present moment is all you ever have. Make the NOW the primary focus of your life." It's up to us to make the most of each moment that we are given. We can't wait for something significant to happen for our life to begin. Life is, after all, nothing more than a series of moments strung together. I purchased a wooden plaque when they were in fashion. The message was, "Enjoy this moment for this moment is your life." That spoke to me because one of my past weaknesses was moving too fast and missing out on many of life's precious moments. Oprah Winfrey states, "My philosophy is doing the best at this moment puts you in the best place for the next moment".

Self-awareness is a significant component in the quest for self-organization. Mindfulness through meditation seems to be an excellent practice in pursuit of self-awareness. Mindful meditation teaches us to be unconditionally present and in the moment. Find a quiet spot and let your mind wander. There is no need to follow a pattern or think a certain way. This type of meditation is nothing more than being you, alone with your thoughts, and letting those thoughts wander. When we are mindful, we are able to fully enjoy the moments of our lives. Treat yourself to a few minutes of peace and quiet in an otherwise-hectic day. Take a stroll and enjoy the stillness, or if that's not enough, run until you get into the "zone." Breathe, free your mind, and simply "be." Do whatever you need to do to relax and savor each moment.

My cousin hosted an extraordinary family reunion in the Florida Keys. We spent several unforgettable days connecting with relatives from all across the country. One afternoon, about forty members of the clan embarked on a kayaking trip through the mangroves. I was enjoying skimming over the water, exploring the everglades, lost in the natural beauty. The younger me could easily have been engaged in conversation for the entire adventure and missed the beauty in the small things. The newer in-the-moment me was making memories, relishing the remarkable flora and fauna.

Everyone is wired a little differently. My brain allows me to work on projects in fifteen-minute increments and then stop and move on to the next task. By chipping away on projects and life a mere fifteen minutes at a time, one of two things happen. Some projects gain momentum as they progress and finish with a flourish, in a timely manner. More challenging situations require working through the job by committing to consistent, short intervals until the job is complete. The first scenario offers more enjoyment of the process and pride in the execution, but the second one gets the job done, too.

For some people, small bites are difficult. These are the people who start a book and stay up all night reading it, whether or not the book is worthy of overindulgence. I have always been an avid reader, but the last time I recall reading a book in one sitting (airplanes not included) was about forty years ago. Truman Capote's *In Cold Blood* (1965) was riveting. I consistently read several chapters a day, which amounts to forty or fifty books annually. If you have never been a reader, try committing to a minimum of ten pages a day. Once it becomes a habit, you will work your way through about one book each month. Reading enriches our lives in countless ways. I highly recommend finding a genre that interests you and begin reading, or listening to, books on a regular basis. The small-bite routine will enhance all areas of your life. Consistent practice alters your behavior, little by little forms life habits, and in time will rewire your brain.

It works if you start small. I know some very successful Realtors who after many years in the business have still not created a database of clients. Why? They claim that they don't have the time to spend to review their entire career in order to build one. My response to that is, start today with what you have and add a few names per day, every day. Your client base is a work in progress. It will never be complete if you are working your business properly and meeting new prospects on a regular basis. It will feel less like a burden if you take small, incremental steps daily. Once you habitually do the things you need to do, your life and your business become organized and you get more done. It sounds simple, but it takes focused attention on a regular basis to get to that point.

In the same way that reading a few pages or adding a few names to your database gets you to the goal, doing anything for a few minutes every day moves you forward, and over time, makes a difference. Consider starting now to save for retirement. According to Atul Gawande in his book *Being Mortal*, the US population today is made up of as many fifty-year-olds as five-year-olds. He contends that in thirty short years, there will be as many people over eighty as there are under five. That's certainly cause for concern when you consider all of the people who are over fifty today who have not prepared for retirement. If your current plan is to "work until you drop"—a plan I have heard from more than a few people—you might want to give that a little more thought. Working until your dying day would not be a bad thing, providing you enjoy what you are doing. However, without the safety net of a retirement plan, it would be alarming to be infirm and unable to earn a living.

I was lucky enough to meet and work with an excellent and competent financial planner. He advised me to start saving money, small amounts at a time with a plan in place to step up the process as my career prospered. I learned early to allow professionals to guide me in areas that are outside my area of expertise. Financial planning is one of those areas, so I followed his advice with blind faith. It's possible to start with a few dollars, and by funding your account consistently, set yourself up for the most important asset in your later years—peace of mind. The Rule of 72 will give you a feel for how fast your savings will grow. Divide the number 72 by the expected annual return of your investment. The result will indicate the number of years it will take to double your money. Once you become familiar with the power and the thrill of compounding interest, saving for the future becomes a very enjoyable game. You may have heard this anonymous quote before: "Do something today that your future self will thank you for." It speaks to many areas of our lives, but is spot-on when it comes to financial planning for the future.

Author Simon Sinek assures us that "it doesn't matter when we start, it doesn't matter where we start, all that matters is that we start" (2015). Don't wait for the stars to align to design the life you want to live. Be disciplined, focused, and committed right now. The famous novelist Agatha Christie further encourages, "The secret to getting ahead is getting started". There is no time like the present to become a better version of you. Get started now.

Fifteen

Living with an Attitude of Gratitude

"Develop an attitude of gratitude, and give thanks for everything that happens to you, knowing that every step forward is a step toward achieving something bigger and better than your current situation."

— BRIAN TRACY, SPEAKER, AUTHOR, AND SUCCESS EXPERT

Y ou don't have to show up for every argument you are invited to. Pick your battles. Some people are argumentative and actually seem to thrive on confrontation. I can and do stand up for myself or for people and ideas that are important to me. The problem is that it's not my nature, and the aftershock of an argument leaves me with an "anger hangover." I walk away feeling headachy and tired. My opponent never even seems fazed—just another day in the life...

I carefully avoid taking a stand unless my side of the argument is based on very solid ground. A personal rule requires thinking about what is bothering me for one full day before speaking up. If I still feel upset the following day, it's not just a case of overreacting or being emotional. It's time to speak up and voice my feelings. Another technique, which facilitates taking a stand without confrontational interaction, is to commit your side of the argument to writing. This helps you express your feelings by focusing only on the recent difficulty or misunderstanding that has you wound up. It prevents you from becoming mired in past transgressions and offers a civilized way to present your side. If you follow the twenty-four-hour rule and you are no longer upset the next day, shred the letter and don't dwell on the situation any longer. However, if you still feel you have a valid point, send it and stand your ground.

A very good friend of mine has worked in several offices that I have managed during my career. She reminded me that a long time ago I taught her a wonderful life lesson. She was up in arms about a situation that she felt was wrong, but because it was out of her control, she wasn't able to correct it. I asked her one question that smoothed her ruffled feathers: "Do you want to be right or do you want to be happy?" Concentrate on the solution, instead of placing blame or trying to impress everyone with what you know. If you need to step up to protect your clients or loved ones, do so without hesitation. If you just feel the need to be right "on principle," shake it off and move on. There are so many more positive ways to direct your energy.

Have you ever experienced the emotion that comes when you are feeling satisfied with life until someone shares their excitement about something amazing that just "fell in their lap"? It feels as though we struggle for every little step forward and others enjoy the benefit of a windfall. When this happens, it's easy to be sincerely happy for people you respect and admire. It's not as easy to be happy for the ones you made a conscious effort to distance yourself from to allow more white space in your life.

There is a simple solution to the problem. Instead of begrudging their success, take the high road. It can be difficult at times to remain gracious in the face of disappointment. We're human. The best way to get past resentment is to step up and congratulate the other person on their success as soon as possible. There is freedom in taking the initiative to sincerely applaud them on their recent win. They will certainly appreciate your congratulations, but the real reward comes from the gratifying feeling you enjoy by being the bigger person. Learn to be authentically happy when good things happen to others. You will feel good about yourself and able to put the situation behind you. Don't worry, your time will come.

As expressed in chapter 2, "Start at the Core of the Matter," gratitude is one of my core values. I choose to live a life of gratitude even though my life has not always been perfect. In 2011 I was diagnosed with cancer and my otherwise-happy, healthy existence was shattered. The diagnosis was leiomyosarcoma, an aggressive and very rare form of cancer. I immediately searched the web and armed myself with as much information as possible, researching every article written and every study conducted regarding leiomyosarcoma. There wasn't much data available and the little that I found was grim. When something sounded hopeful or interesting it was forwarded to my oncologist along with a barrage of questions for which there were no good answers. Cancer is not just a disease of the body. It's a disease of the mind and spirit as well. If I allowed myself to dwell on the problem without a plan of action, the anxiety would consume me, sending my mind into overdrive, weakening my spirit, and hindering the healing of my body. That's how I acknowledged it: mind-spirit-body, as one. I became a cancer warrior and began the fight for my life.

It was necessary to resign myself to the fact that cancer would define me during this time, but I vowed that it would not define me as a person. I took a holistic approach and waged battles on every front. To ensure that everything possible was being done physically, I sought second opinions, enlisted the help of a nutritionist, tried herbal treatments, organic food supplements, and folk remedies. My diet was primarily plant based and alkaline water became my drink of choice. I sought help spiritually by visiting a healing room and by adding my name to every prayer list possible. I explored the metaphysical aspect because we don't know what we don't know and there is so much that is beyond our understanding. I carried a specially made hologram at all times in hopes that it would change how energy interacted with the resources in my body to allow it to heal itself. No stone was unturned. I pushed my doctors on every level. If they recommended three weeks post-surgery recovery before starting chemotherapy, I campaigned successfully for two. When my blood levels were too low to tolerate chemo infusions, we compromised by scheduling four hours of blood transfusions followed by four hours of chemotherapy. This tirelessly proactive battle was exhausting for everyone, but there is no doubt that advocating for my life in this manner attracted attention, on earth and in heaven, and made all the difference.

I share the story of my cancer journey to provide insight to others in an effort to calm fear of the unknown and to offer hope to you, or someone you know, fighting an overwhelming battle. Cancer does not have to win. Take a stand, fight the good fight and don't let the bad guys win. If you know someone who would benefit from the story of this modern-day miracle, the unabridged version is available on my blog www.cancercandor.com.

I have been cancer free for two years as of this writing and I am eternally grateful. When fighting the illness, I made a conscious and purposeful decision to step up my gratitude of life and to carry myself with grace and dignity, thanking God for everything and everyone in my life. Every day begins and ends with an accounting of my substantial blessings, which fills my spirit with gratitude. It has not always been easy, but even when it's difficult, I give thanks, recognize the positive, and remain an eternal optimist. That spirit of gratitude continued during and after my treatments. These days, my gratitude journal overflows with lists of people and things that I am thankful for every day.

Our minds can focus on only one emotion at a time. When we think happy thoughts, it is virtually impossible to simultaneously think negative thoughts. This concentrated, positive effort worked for me and became my saving grace. Once my mind was focused on the good, my spirit was right behind. There has not been one day since that time that I haven't found hundreds of instances during my waking hours to give thanks. When insomnia strikes, counting and recounting my blessings becomes the peaceful precursor to sleep.

The cancer event required reprioritizing my life. Time outside of business is now spent primarily with family and a handful of close friends. In the pre-cancer past, I wasn't as jealous of my time and agreed to do things that didn't really interest me, with people who were not particularly important in my life. Now that I have been given a second chance, I'm determined to get it right. I avoid spreading myself too thin: family first, with a select few friends peppered in as time permits. Living in gratitude keeps my mind-spirit-body healthy, happy, and content. As a result, I have become a better version of me.

Counting your blessings is the best way to start and/or end your day. Many speakers and coaches encourage the use of gratitude journals. They usually suggest listing ten things you are thankful for and ten intentions daily. I simply open my journal and replay the day. My stream of consciousness takes the lead and the gratitude flows—sometimes more than ten, sometimes fewer, but always very gratifying. Much of the joy comes from the little things, which become bigger things when you take the time to appreciate them.

Remember, "thoughts are things." This habit will manifest an abundance of goodness in your life.

Today I am grateful for

_____

_____

_____

_____

_____

_____

_____

_____

I want to thank

_____

_____

_____

_____

_____

I will make a difference by

_____

_____

_____

_____

_____

_____

_____

_____

Self-Actualization

✓ Follow your dream
✓ Upgrade your life
✓ Believe you can
✓ Be the best version
of you

Sixteen

Live the Life You Want to Live

"What a man can be, he must be. This need
we call self-actualization."

— ABRAHAM MASLOW (1943)

Maslow's Hierarchy of Needs was introduced in his
1943 paper "A Theory of Human Motivation." Maslow
states that people are motivated by basic needs rather than
by rewards or desires. He identifies five areas where a person is motivated to fulfill those needs, believing that only
when the first need is fulfilled, a person is motivated to pursue the next level. It begins with the most basic physiologi-
cal essentials: air to breathe, food, drink, shelter, warmth,
and sleep. Once these needs are met, a person has the
energy to fulfill the next level of desires. Level two per-
tains to a need for safety: law and order, protection from

the elements, and security. When a person feels safe and secure, there comes a need for togetherness, love, family, friends, and relationships. The fourth level deals with self-respect and self-esteem, the need for status, and the emotions that come with achievement and success. People are not overly concerned about prestige when they are hungry. First things first.

The first four levels are referred to as "deficiency needs." If you don't satisfy these needs, they further deteriorate until they are satisfied. For example, if you don't eat, you get hungrier; if you don't sleep, you get sleepier; if you're cold, you get colder. Only after a person has met and fulfilled his or her deficiency needs is he or she able to concentrate on level five, which Maslow identified as self-actualization.

Self-actualization has been defined as "the achievement of one's full potential through creativity, independence, spontaneity, and a grasp of the real world." That's what I'm talking about. This level represents the desire to accomplish everything possible and to become the most that you can be. It's not only understanding your full potential, but also realizing that potential by being the person you were meant to be. The first part of this book dealt with many facets of self-organization. The more together you can be, the more actualized your life will become. If you put plans in place based on what you have read so far, your goals are set. Daily schedules are in place, you live and work consistently, and procrastination is a thing of the past. You have created time and energy for all that life offers and are in position to identify what you want out of life and go after it. Build a bucket list, or even better, build a life list! Bill Clinton warns that "when our memories outweigh our dreams we have grown old". A life lived fully with passion and purpose will become your own personal fountain of youth!

David Brooks, author of *The Road to Character* (2015), conveys the message brilliantly. He says, "Sit down and take some time to discover yourself, to define what is really important to you, what your priorities are, what arouses your deepest passions. You should ask certain questions: What is the purpose of my life? What do I want from life? What are the things that I truly value, that are not done just to please or impress the people around me?" Start by listing your interests and talents, things that excite you. Set goals and benchmarks to track your progress and focus on the results you are seeking. Brooks further states, "It's a method that starts with the self and ends with the self, which begins with self-investigation and ends in self-fulfillment. This is a life determined by a series of choices." That's another way of saying, when you master self-organization, you will have created a life of self-actualization.

I have referenced your hopes and dreams at several points in this book. Have you started to think about what you would like to experience in your lifetime? Don't wait until the moment is perfect. If you postpone truly living until X happens, you will miss out on the beauty along the way and the opportunities that surround you daily. How many times have we heard about a person who spent his or her life working hard, finally reaching retirement age ready to start enjoying his or her life, when he or she passed away? There are too many to count, and even one is too many. Your self-actualization or bucket list is a work in progress. If you stay in curious mode, you will continually be adding new adventures and opportunities to your life list. According to Oprah Winfrey, "The biggest adventure you can take is to live the life of your dreams".

I have led a very full life, rich with memories. Travel has been a passion of mine for decades. Here are a few travel experiences that have changed my life:

I have

- ✓ spent several days with my brother in Bangkok when he was on R & R during the Vietnam War;
- ✓ visited Hong Kong when it was a British territory and again many years later after it reverted back to China;
- ✓ walked the ancient streets of Ephesus, Turkey, and visited the very holy house of the Virgin Mary;
- ✓ kissed the Blarney Stone;
- ✓ traveled to the top of the Empire State Building, the Eiffel Tower, and the Space Needle;
- ✓ viewed the *Mona Lisa* in Paris, Michelangelo's *David* in Florence, and the Sistine Chapel in Rome;
- ✓ enjoyed glorious cherry blossom in Washington, DC, and Tokyo;
- ✓ visited Mahatma Gandhi's home in Bombay (Mumbai);
- ✓ climbed to the top of the Teotihuacán pyramids in Mexico City;

- ✓ experienced the grandeur of the Grand Canyon and Niagara Falls;
- ✓ snorkeled in the Great Barrier Reef;
- ✓ toured the Sydney Opera House;
- ✓ soared in a hot air balloon at the Albuquerque International Balloon Fiesta;
- ✓ enjoyed a production of Les Ballets Africains in Senegal;
- ✓ stood under a waterfall in Kuala Lumpur, Malaysia;
- ✓ crossed the English Channel via the Chunnel;
- ✓ visited Stonehenge, the Leaning Tower of Pisa, and the Colosseum;
- ✓ celebrated Mass at the Vatican;
- ✓ shopped the vibrant souks of Marrakech, Morocco;
- ✓ crossed the equator and earned membership in The Neptune Society;
- ✓ hiked Table Mountain in Cape Town, South Africa;
- ✓ participated in a big game camera safari in Kenya;
- ✓ zip-lined over the rain forests of Costa Rica;
- ✓ given thanks with my son and other US soldiers in Frankfurt, Germany, on Thanksgiving Day;
- ✓ treasured the beauty and the love story of the Taj Mahal in Agra, India;
- ✓ celebrated Joya no Kane (the most important holiday in Japan), the sacred tolling of temple bells on New Year's Eve in Kyoto;
- ✓ honeymooned in Budapest and Prague; and
- ✓ cruised through the Panama Canal.

I have visited more than forty countries and six of the seven continents and have certainly enjoyed life. Rather than getting shorter, my list is continually being updated and altered. It grows longer by the day. H. Jackson Brown Jr., the author of *Life's Little Instruction Book*, says, "Twenty years from now you will be more disappointed by the things you didn't do than by the ones you did. So throw off the bowlines. Sail away from the safe harbor. Catch the trade winds in your sails. Explore. Dream. Discover." Always have something to look forward and aspire to. There are so many dreams that are worth chasing that it's impossible to list them all. Here are a few ideas to bring your vision to life and inspire you to recognize what you would like to achieve or experience in your lifetime:

- Visit the seven continents or the seven seas.
- Visit all fifty states of the United States.
- Write a book.
- See the Seven Wonders of the World.
- Run a marathon.
- Climb a mountain.
- View the aurora borealis.
- Start your own business.
- Learn to play a musical instrument.
- Go to the Olympics, the Super Bowl, or World Series.
- Bungee jump, hang glide, or skydive.
- Learn to sail, ski, or snowboard.
- Run for office.
- Volunteer or donate your hair to Locks of Love.

- Start a blog.
- Learn a new language.

The list is endless. If you need more inspiration, google *bucket list*. The wealth of imaginative ideas will astound you. If you see anything that resonates with you, add it to your own list. Spend a little time investing in self-discovery. When you take charge of your life, you will enhance your self-esteem, express genuine joy, and find your true purpose. Push yourself outside of your comfort zone and give some serious thought to the following questions:

- What would you do if you won the lottery?
- What activities and skills do you want to learn?
- If you knew your death was imminent, what would you do before you die?
- What are your deepest hopes and wildest dreams?
- What would you want to achieve?
- What would come under the heading of "woulda, coulda, shoulda"?
- What would you like to share with the people you care about?
- How do you want to be remembered?

It has been said that I am a lucky person. This may be true, but I don't count on the universe to shape my life. I make my own luck by establishing goals, creating strategies to achieve them, and committing to whatever it takes to accomplish them. Self-organization is the necessary first step to a self-actualized life. There are no shortcuts. It requires hard work, focus, and discipline to manifest a self-actualized life. As luck would have it, the harder I work, the luckier I get. I continue to grow personally and enrich my life by committing to lifelong learning and have flourished as a result of my never-ending self-improvement campaign. I give daily thanks for the opportunities that life has gifted me. At the same time, I recognize and express tremendous gratitude for the opportunities that would have been missed had I not passionately pursued them with energy and commitment to a self-organized life.

Commit right now to start living every day as if it were your last. It may sound clichéd, but that is one thing that is out of our control. Let the people you love know it. Mend fences where needed. Remember, you don't always have to be right. Learn to let things go and enjoy a little happiness. Make and savor wonderful memories, be fully present in every moment, and appreciate the now along the way. My hope is that you will revisit the chapters that spoke to you and focus on just one small change that you wish to make in your current life. Break it down and create systems to make the change manageable. Commit to working on it consistently until it becomes a habit for life. And then repeat the process again, and then again. Once you have created a life that truly reflects who you are and aligns with your core values, you will have become a better person than you were before, living the life you want to live.

My wish for you is that you always have more dreams than memories. Stretch yourself to self-actualize all that you are meant to be. Start now to create the life that up until now you may not even have dreamed of, and become a better version of you.

Here's some paper. Grab a pen and begin today to build the life of your dreams!

Expressing Gratitude

"Feeling gratitude and not expressing it is
like wrapping a present and not giving it."

— WILLIAM ARTHUR WARD, AUTHOR OF
FOUNTAIN OF FAITH

I would like to express my sincere gratitude to the many supporters who cheered me on through the writing of this book. So many of you offered enthusiastic support by reading, editing, and offering candid insight to ensure that it was the best version it could be. Thanks to those of you who reminded me of favorite anecdotes that you wanted included in the book. Special thanks to Steve Price, Nancy McCracken, Stephanie Walling, and John Karelius for proofreading and helping to smooth the very rough edges of the first drafts. Thanks to Jane Lippman for providing the inspiration needed to complete the final few details. And finally, heartfelt thanks to John Archuleta for the creative graphics.

Bibliography

Quotations by celebrities or historic figures are referenced with the website sources where they can be found. These links will provide you with further information.

Andretti, Mario. BrainyQuote.com, Xplore Inc, 2015. http://www.brainyquote.com/quotes/quotes/m/marioandre130613.html, accessed May 5, 2015.

Aristotle. BrainyQuote.com, Xplore Inc, 2015. http://www.brainyquote.com/quotes/quotes/a/aristotle145967.html, accessed March 3, 2015.

Breathnach, Sarah Ban. *Simple Abundance: A Daybook of Comfort and Joy*. New York: Warner Books, Inc., 1995.

Brooks, David. *The Road to Character*. New York: Random House, 2015.

Brown, Brene. *Daring Greatly*. New York: Penguin Group, 2012.

Brown Jr., H. Jackson. *Life's Little Instruction Book*. Nashville: Thomas Nelson Publishing, 1988.

Bruckner, Jerry. *The Success Formula for Personal Growth*. Stamford: BRIJU Publishing, 2010.

Capote, Truman. *In Cold Blood*. New York: Random House, 1966.

Christie, Agatha. http://www.goodreads.com/quotes/ 394975-the-secret-of-getting-ahead-is-getting-started, accessed May 10, 2015

Clason, George S. *The Richest Man in Babylon*. New York: Penguin Books, 1989.

Clinton, William. Goodreads http://www.goodreads. com/quotes/583574-when-our-memories-outweigh- our-dreams-we-have-grown-old, accessed March 20, 2015.

Confucius. BrainyQuote.com, Xplore Inc, 2015. http://www. brainyquote.com/quotes/quotes/c/confucius104563. html, accessed February 18, 2015.

Covey, Stephen. *The Seven Habits of Highly Effective People*. New York: RosettaBooks, 1989.

Emerson, Ralph Waldo. BrainyQuote.com, Xplore Inc, 2015.p http://www.brainyquote.com/quotes/quotes/r/ ralphwaldo387459.html, accessed March 15, 2015.

Firebaugh, Doug. All Famous Quotes. http://www.all- famous-quotes.com/Doug_Firebaugh_quotes.html, assessed April 2014

Ford, Henry. Forbes. Erika Anderson. http://www.forbes.com/sites/erikaandersen/2013/05/31/21-quotes-from-henry-ford-on-business-leadership-and-life/ , accessed January 3, 2015

Gandhi, Mahatma. Goodreads http://www.goodreads.com/quotes/50584-your-beliefs-become-your-thoughts-your-thoughts-become-your-words

BrainyQuote   http://www.brainyquote.com/quotes/quotes/m/mahatmagan133995.html, accessed March, 2015.

Garland, Judy. Goodreads Judy Garland Quotes www.goodreads.com/.../5466-always-be-a-better-version-of-yourself-and-not-a-second-rate-version-of-some-one-else, accessed August 7, 2014

Garst, Kim. Goodreads http://www.goodreads.com/quotes/1046224-my-name-is-consistency-i-am-related-to-success-we, accessed September 20, 2014

Gawande, Atul. *Being Mortal.* New York: Metropolitan Books, 2014

———. *The Checklist Manifesto.* New York: Metropolitan Books, 2009

Godin, Seth. *Linchpin.* New York: The Penguin Group, 2010

Greenleaf, Robert K. *Servant as Leader*. New York: Paulist Press, 2002

Hansen, Mark Victor. Goodreads. http://www. goodreads.com/quotes/100005-don-t-wait-until-everything-is-just-right-it-will-never, accessed April 2, 2015

Iacocca, Lee. *Lee Iacocca* by Lee Iacocca and William Novak. New York: Bantam Books, 1984

Lombardi, Vince. BrainyQuote.com, Xplore Inc, 2015. http://www.brainyquote.com/quotes/quotes/v/ vincelomba121318.html, accessed March 18, 2014.

Mandino, Og. BrainyQuote.com, Xplore Inc, 2015. http:// www.brainyquote.com/quotes/quotes/o/ogmandi-no133544.html, accessed May 15, 2015.

Mariboli, Steve. *Life, the Truth, and Being Free*. Port Washington: A Better Today Publishing, 2009.

Maslow, Abraham. "A Theory of Human Motivation." Washington, D.C.: Psychological Review, 1943.

Passoff, Michelle. *Lighten Up!: Free Yourself from Clutter*. New York: William Morrow Paperbacks, 1998.

Powell, Colin. BrainyQuote.com, Xplore Inc, 2015. http://www.brainyquote.com/quotes/quotes/c/colinpowel138130.html, accessed May 8, 2015.

Richards, Stephen. *Overcoming Procrastination.* Northampton: Mirage Publishing, 2011.

Rogers, Will. Attributed to Will Rogers

Rohn, Jim. The Treasury of Quotes. Lake Dallas: Success Books, 1994

Ross, Diana. "I Am Me." *Silk Electric Album*, RCA, 1982.

Rufus, Allan. *The Master's Sacred Knowledge.* North Charleston: CreateSpace, 2012.

Schuller, Robert H. BrainyQuote.com, Xplore Inc, 2015. http://www.brainyquote.com/quotes/quotes/r/roberthsc107582.html, accessed March 18, 2014.

Shaw, George Bernard. En*Theos https://www.entheos.com/quotes/by_topic/George+Bernard+Shaw accessed May, 2015

Silver, Spencer. Wikipedia. https://en.wikipedia.org/wiki/Post-it_note, accessed April, 18, 2015

Sinek, Simon. *Start with Why*. New York: Penguin Publishing Group, 2009

Thoreau, Henry David. Goodreads http://www.goodreads.com/quotes/278883-go-confidently-in-the-direction-of-your-dreams-live-the

Tolle, Eckhart. *The Power of NOW: A Guide to Spiritual Enlightenment*. Novato: New World Library, 2001.

Tracy, Brian. BrainyQuote.com, Xplore Inc, 2015. http://www.brainyquote.com/quotes/quotes/b/briantracy125860.html, accessed March 17, 2015.

van der Rohe, Mies. BrainyQuote.com, Xplore Inc, 2015. http://www.brainyquote.com/quotes/quotes/l/ludwigmies116038.html, accessed March 7, 2015.

Ward, William Arthur. BrainyQuote.com, Xplore Inc, 2015. http://www.brainyquote.com/quotes/quotes/w/williamart105516.html, accessed June 17, 2014.

Winfrey, Oprah. BrainyQuote.com, Xplore Inc, 2015. http://www.brainyquote.com/quotes/quotes/o/oprahwinfr383916.html, accessed March 16, 2015.

Zuckerberg, Mark. Stone, Brad and Frier, Sarah. Facebook Turns 10: The Mark Zuckerberg Interview. Bloomberg Business. January 30, 2014, accessed February 2, 2015.

About the Author

After thirty-six years in the business of real estate, Martha Karelius decided it was time to reposition herself from successful Realtor and corporate executive to sharing what she has learned to help others succeed. Throughout her career, Martha was the recipient of numerous awards and built an exemplary reputation as an agent, trainer, and speaker. She has extensive experience in management, serving at the branch level, and in later years, at the corporate level.

Martha is real, down to earth, and relatable. Her fast-paced style not only educates, but also motivates and inspires her audience. She is an advocate of a balanced, joy-filled life and consistently works to improve her talents and abilities in both business and life. This book is not designed to transform you. Martha recognizes that each of us is blessed with unique personal strengths. Her objective is to help you acknowledge those gifts and inspire you to be a better version of you.

Made in the USA
San Bernardino, CA
07 October 2015